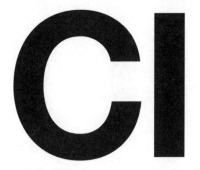

Cultural Intelligence

the art of leading
cultural complexity

Elisabeth Plum

in collaboration with
Benedikte Achen
Inger Dræby
Iben Jensen

Middlesex
University
PRESS

First published in 2008 by Middlesex University Press

Copyright © Elisabeth Plum

ISBN 978 1 904750 61 1

A CIP catalogue record for this book is available from The British Library

Design by Helen Taylor based on an original design by Olga Bramsen
Printed and bound by Cambridge Printing, UK
Illustrations by Benedikte Achen

Danish version first published in 2007 by Børsens Forlag, Denmark

Translation by Hanne and Ian Bock, Sprog & Data, Denmark

Middlesex University Press
The Burroughs
London
NW4 4BT
Tel: +44 (0)20 8411 4162
Fax: +44 (0)20 8411 4167
www.mupress.co.uk

Mixed Sources
Product group from well-managed forests and other controlled sources
www.fsc.org Cert no. SA-COC-1527
© 1996 Forest Stewardship Council

Contents

Introduction

Culture and cultural differences have a greater influence on business effectiveness than we think and it is therefore important for companies to develop the cultural intelligence of their employees.

As organisations become more global, mergers and strategic alliances become more common, developing the skills to get the best from different cultures becomes a necessity rather than an option – and we are not only thinking about the national differences between people. Innovation, knowledge sharing, and creative problem solving demand collaboration across boundaries of different professions, job functions and organisations, and these activities depend on people's ability to work with people who think and act differently from themselves.

The cultural challenge faced by companies 20 years ago was often simply to prepare individuals to go abroad and work and negotiate effectively in a foreign national culture. But today's global and knowledge-intensive companies are faced with a much more challenging cultural complexity involving many key people both at home and in subsidiaries, outsourcing companies and sub-contractors. Not only is the organisation itself often home to and carrier of several professional, national and organisational cultures but the employers are at the same time also working with business partners from other organisations and countries.

The challenges and problems of culturally complex organisations cannot be solved using the thinking of past generations. We need to develop new mindsets and models. We need to see difference in a new way, where interdependence is a given, and where working with difference is a competitive advantage rather than an obstacle to be worked around.

This book explains the concept of cultural intelligence and presents a different angle from which to look at and approach other cultures, as well as some practical approaches for coming to grips with the somewhat intangible concept of culture. Cultural intelligence is defined as the ability to make oneself understood and the ability to create a fruitful collaboration in situations where cultural differences play a role.

We offer a new way in which to look at and approach culture. We argue that the same cultural dynamics are at play whether we look at professional, organisational or national differences. This viewpoint allows a broad approach to culture as well as the transfer of cross-cultural experiences from one field to another. Our approach is based on a dynamic concept of culture, seeing culture as a dynamic and socially constructed phenomenon rather than a fixed set of rules, and suggests ways to benefit from cultural differences using them as resources and a route to innovation.

This book's concept of cultural intelligences has been developed in a Scandinavian context. However, the models and theories span a wide variety of sources from different national contexts: the USA, UK, France, The Netherlands, Canada, Chile, and Singapore. Our model comes from theories which define organisations as complex adaptive systems that rely on a constant flow of information in all directions. It is not a hierarchical model where the top of the pyramid has the knowledge and the information to make decisions on behalf of others. In this model the organisation is expected to learn in order to adapt and equality is assumed even though there are power differences between people depending on their role. To do this we have to treat others with respect and an open mind even though they do not think or react like 'us'.

As a type of intelligence, cultural intelligence is broader in scope than both emotional and social intelligence, insofar as it reveals itself in the ability to create understanding between several types of culture at the individual as well as the organisational level. Cultural intelligence comprises three interdependent elements: an emotional, a knowledge-based and a practical element, and it is thus something else, and more than, intercultural competence. The three dimensions are equally essential – together they provide a deeper understanding of cultural dynamics, including the emotional drives and irrational reactions which occur when differences meet. Cultural intelligence offers an overview of what happens in cultural encounters and provides inspiration for more options for action – for it is important to find new ways of talking about culture and cultural differences out there in the local and global workplaces.

Chapter 1 presents the concept of cultural intelligence with its three elements, and describes how these three elements affect each other. Examples of culturally intelligent practice and its opposite are presented, and finally, cultural intelligence is compared with other broad concepts of intelligence.

Chapter 2 contains the groundwork, defining culture and its importance in various contexts, and arguing in favour of a complex understanding of culture in which culture is seen as a process. This is in contrast to the traditional descriptive approach, which sees culture as a firm nucleus within man. Communication across cultural differences is explored, and the chapter finishes with a discussion of the consequences of focusing too much or too little on the question of culture.

Next follow three theme chapters, each of which provides an in-depth discussion of one cultural field of pressing importance for private and public organisations. These chapters will focus on one cultural difference at a time, as if a cultural dimension appears in isolation in pure form – which it never does. A cultural dimension will always be part of a complexity where more than one dimension affects the communication, and we ask the reader to bear this in mind. All three theme chapters offer several ideas and tools for handling the issue in question in a culturally intelligent manner.

Chapter 3 describes professional cultural differences as an important ingredient in knowledge sharing, innovation and cross-disciplinary problem solving, although professional cultures often receive little attention and a somewhat *ad hoc* handling in the workplace. This chapter discusses the concept of professionalism and the function of professional cultures, and we present a model illustrating different types of cross-professional cooperation. We pinpoint some of the factors which lift professional partnerships up to a level above that of the individual professions, thus promoting better knowledge sharing, innovation and cross-disciplinary problem solving.

Chapter 4 focuses on the cultural dimensions of mergers and on how the cultural integration is often up and running before management is aware of it. What happens when the company is to 'marry' the 'enemy' or the 'neighbour', or be integrated into a large unit? Management's role in the merger process is discussed, and the concept of an organisational culture as a unified culture is refuted. This chapter explains the importance of cultural differences in achieving a good result, and the fact that cultural differences should not be used as an easy explanation of problems of merging.

Chapter 5 focuses on cross-national relations in a company, but it is also relevant for external partnerships between companies from different countries and national cultures. Relations between nationalities are an area which is highly charged with stereotypes, and this chapter discusses the importance of national self-perception and pre-perceptions, and how to act in a culturally intelligent manner in cross-national multicultural encounters. The chapter discusses various models of 'cultural mapping' for promoting understanding between different nationalities, and how to relate to the general patterns in various cultures without becoming trapped in stereotypical perceptions.

Chapter 6 contains an overview of the CI concept and a general discussion of how to develop cultural intelligence. What type of learning will develop CI, and what are the important principles in this development? The chapter considers how individuals can develop their cultural intelligence as well as how the development of cultural intelligence can be tackled on an organisational basis, and how to use the models and tools from the theme chapters in other cultural fields.

The book is aimed at managers and key people in staff development, project management, cross-national partnerships, merger management and innovation.

The book is the result of a collaborative effort of the four authors. Elisabeth Plum conceived the idea for the book and is the main architect behind the concept of cultural intelligence, and she wrote Chapers 1, 4 and 6, and Chapter 2 with Iben Jensen, while Benedikte Achen wrote Chapter 3 and Inger Dræby Chapter 5.

We ask the reader to see our book as part of a continuous

development process since we will elaborate this approach further according to our experiences from helping people leading cultural complexity in different organisations and various cultural fields.

The book contains many examples, methods and models, and is written on the basis of the authors' teaching, research and consultancy work in Denmark and abroad over more than 20 years. It utilises experiences gained from work on the development of international groups from diversity projects, cross-disciplinary project management in various sectors, and mergers and other organisational developments. It includes experiences and examples from the authors' partnerships with numerous private companies and public organisations. We wish to thank all of you who thus, voluntarily or unwittingly, contributed ideas and material for this book.

We are grateful for the financial and professional support we received from Middlesex University Business School for this English version of our book, and for the professional advice and help provided by MU Press. We owe special thanks to our friend and colleague Dympna Cunnane for her untiring encouragement and wise counsel.

1/

CULTURAL INTELLIGENCE

Cultural intelligence is judged on the results of a meeting of cultures, not on the participants' intentions or thoughts

Let us imagine that somebody asks you to dance, and that you are moving on to the dance floor with your partner in the belief that you know this dance. But it only takes a few steps for you to realise that something is wrong. Your movements are not at one with your partner's, and you don't follow the music and each other as you'd expected. Your partner's rhythm and body movements are different from yours, and you feel that you're often about to step on each other's toes. Your movements are awkward and staccato, and you're becoming embarrassingly conscious of the spectacle the two of you must be presenting to onlookers. You want to dance together, so neither of you will take the initiative and leave the dance floor. You laugh apologetically to each other and try hard to find a rhythm that suits you both. Your body is super-attentive to your partner's movements in your attempt to find steps that will allow you to move together with the music. Finally you succeed in finding a pattern of movement that suits you both. It isn't the dance you first expected, and probably not the one your partner imagined either. Perhaps you just invented your own merged dance for the occasion. The sense of embarrassment disappears. You're able to relax more, and you're moving together with the music.

How do two people manage such a situation? It happens through a process of unspoken synchronisation arising out of their understanding of dancing and music, their motivation to dance together, and their willingness to try. This situation on the dance floor has many points in common with a cross-cultural encounter in which doubts and misunderstandings arise because the two parties have different views of the situation and different expectations of what should happen. The response you get may be different from the one you expect, and it makes you uncertain as to the other party's intentions. If a cross-cultural encounter is to be constructive and fruitful, both parties must bring their cultural intelligence into play, and this is very similar to what happened in the dance.

What is cultural intelligence?

Cultural intelligence (CI) is the ability to act appropriately in situations where cultural differences are important, and the ability to make yourself understood and to establish a constructive partnership across cultural differences. Cultural intelligence is judged on the results of the encounter, not on the participants' intentions or thoughts. An intelligent result of a cross-cultural encounter is the creation of a shared understanding across all the participant cultures – an understanding which will enable the parties to get on with their work. This book will focus on cultural encounters in the workplace, but the theory and the methods can also be used in other social situations.

The concept of cultural intelligence used here is inspired by an American concept but further developed to suit a different cultural tradition and a different practical approach. We will return to this difference later in the chapter.

A broad definition of culture is used, including cultures in organisations, work functions, ethnic, professional and national groups within the term. The sheer range of possible applications is thus a clear indication of how important the development of cultural intelligence is when:

- Organisations or units merge, bridges must be built between the various workplace cultures, and a new shared culture and work procedure must be created.
- A multi-disciplinary team must handle conflicts and gain full advantage of their different fields of expertise, work functions, approaches and methods.

- A company engages in international activities and wishes to respect and utilise the different approaches involved.
- Cross-national teams seek results, and wish to avoid misunderstandings and talking at cross-purposes.
- The aim is greater diversity and better cooperation in workplaces with employees of different age groups, nationality, education, gender and ethnic background.

Cultural intelligence offers a framework for understanding and a set of strategies and methods for handling different types of cross-cultural encounters with better results. Cultural intelligence is particularly important in the early stages of such encounters in order to create a fruitful common culture across all differences. But even when the participants have become used to each other and have learned to handle their mutual differences, cultural intelligence is required for handling situations where unexpected differences pop up and create new fracture points.

Cultural intelligence is a broad concept which is related to emotional intelligence and social intelligence, but cultural intelligence is wider than either of these because it sees both feelings and human relations as culturally determined, and not as identical across cultural boundaries. Intelligence can also be defined as the ability to learn (IQ) – an ability which is both genetically determined and affected by conditions in early childhood. Seen as a broad concept of intelligence, cultural intelligence is a set of abilities/skills which can be developed throughout life.

What are the components of cultural intelligence?

Cultural intelligence has three dimensions: intercultural engagement, cultural understanding, and intercultural communication. This tripartite division follows the classic division into emotion, cognition and practice – or heart, mind and muscle.

Having a high CI involves continuous development of your cultural engagement and cultural understanding, as well as a state of preparedness which makes it possible to act appropriately and to create a shared bridge-building culture in a given situation. None of the three dimensions will yield a high cultural intelligence on its own because CI is the synthesis of all three. The level of cultural intelligence is the level of dynamic interaction between the three elements, and one element cannot be singled out from the other two in everyday life.

The separation into three elements is useful in situations where the cultural intelligence of individuals and groups needs developing. This is because separation makes it possible to analyse specific development needs, and thus to target development work at the areas most in need of new knowledge, competences and methods. In the following example, all three were in need of development.

Lars was an independent consultant, at one time connected to an internet-based salary system for small companies. The system was intended to make light work of salary calculations, salary payment and reporting to the tax and pension scheme authorities. One day something went wrong. A deadline for making a payment to the tax authorities had been overlooked. Lars rang the hotline service for help and spoke to a friendly woman who quickly realised what had gone wrong, and how the problem could be solved. She gave Lars thorough instructions in what to do, but Lars did not understand what she was saying because she used a lot of accounting terms. Lars asked her to repeat the instructions, but to use words which he understood. She then repeated the instructions more slowly and in a louder voice, which didn't help Lars at all. When he said that he still didn't understand, she got cross and asked to speak to somebody in his firm who could understand her so she wouldn't sit there wasting her time. At that point the company lost Lars as a customer.

This is an example of a cross-cultural encounter which never became constructive, and which ended with a negative result. The hotline employee failed to show understanding of the fact that she was using a technical language which not everybody would understand. Perhaps she was unable to imagine that some people might not use the same terms that she did? Apart from cultural understanding, she also lacked the motivation to try to explain the problem to Lars in words he would understand. Motivation is part of the intercultural engagement. Perhaps she lacked the ability to speak about her specialty in any other language? She clearly lacked better scope for action in the situation in which she found herself so that she could solve the client's problem – she showed no ability for intercultural communication.

Some people may say that it was her perception of customer service which was at fault, and that it must be management's and the organisation's obligation to ensure that she is trained in this to enable her to provide satisfactory service to all customers. But to say this does not change the issue: it's still about cultural intelligence. The organisation should have prepared the employee for cross-cultural encounters with people from outside the accountancy culture. The target group was precisely small companies which rarely have an accounts department, and where the owner typically handles all functions in person.

In everyday life, the three dimensions of cultural intelligence are thus intermingled, but let's start by looking at them one by one.

1. Intercultural engagement

The engagement dimension in cultural intelligence is about the emotional aspect of the situation, and it constitutes the fuel in a cross-cultural encounter. It is about motivation, attitude to cultural differences, and the courage to allow oneself to change. It is also about the manner in which we are present in an encounter with people who think and act differently from ourselves.

Motivation implies a desire to create results together with people who are different from oneself. There must be a genuine interest in getting the other party to speak and to be understood, as this creates the personal drive and infuses energy into the situation. If the motivation to make a success of the cross-cultural encounter is present, we will invest more in the encounter and not give up easily, even if some things are difficult.

The in-house training department had always appointed its instructors from among the skilled workers in production, but one day, two young university graduates were appointed. The old instructors didn't like the idea, and were not particularly helpful to the two new colleagues. When instruction teams were arranged, the two graduates always ended up together. One of them was very interested in cooperating with two of the experienced production workers because she could hear that they had expertise within a field which interested her and complemented her own. They rejected her approaches politely several times, but she persisted in looking them up in their offices. She showed an interest in their areas, she suggested small joint projects, and she sat next to them at meetings. Gradually she succeeded in making contact, and the three ended by building up a fruitful partnership. But at that stage the second graduate had given up and found another job.

One sometimes experiences an embarrassing silence or an awkward reaction which indicates that somebody is afraid of offending somebody else. Perhaps the conversation is getting close to cultural taboos. In some situations it may be dress code or religion, and in others, for example in relation to a merger, it may be questions of power. We get the feeling that "Oh God, whatever it is, I've put my foot right into it." It takes engagement and curiosity to continue with "So, what do I do now to make contact about whatever it is that's the problem?"

Intercultural engagement is about the ability to handle your emotional reactions and those of others while realising that the reactions may be culturally conditioned, and not mean the same thing to both parties. As cross-cultural encounters move in the cross-field of different understandings of self and others, they can unintentionally get too close to people and provoke emotional reactions, and misunderstandings can occur which make one of the parties close up, or feel cross, misunderstood or embarrassed. What makes us feel angry or hurt is often determined by culture, and the manner in which we show or don't show our emotions will depend on our cultural coding.

It is culturally intelligent to be able to contain the reactions of yourself and others, notice the strength of your feelings and give yourself the opportunity to think and choose your reactions. This means that we must be able in our minds to rise above the desire to defend our own cultural understanding. For example, if keeping eye contact with the person you are talking to is seen as appropriate behaviour in your own culture, the lack of eye contact with a person from a different culture can feel uncomfortable. We may consciously or unconsciously interpret this as rejecting or invasive. It is culturally intelligent to understand the other person's reaction, to be able to let go of one's own immediate emotional reaction and to hold on to the human contact even if it feels awkward.

Intercultural engagement requires emotional maturity and mental flexibility because it is sometimes necessary to look our own prejudices in the eye and revise our own cultural understanding of ourselves, and that can be a challenge for an adult. We must be able to look at ourselves with new eyes, and this is easier if we don't take ourselves too seriously. We have to be able to put a question mark against our understanding of ourselves and search until we find our own blind spots if, for example, we find ourselves in a defensive position with the urge to defend ourselves. We develop our cultural intelligence by seeking new cross-cultural encounters instead of remaining in the comfort of situations which confirm our own views of ourselves.

The engagement dimension requires us to adopt a questioning attitude to cross-cultural encounters and to be open to the possibility of doing things differently as a result of what we learn in the encounter. A learning attitude and a fair amount of curiosity are the most effective way to counter the need to defend oneself. When meeting colleagues in the newly merged company for the first time, a strong wish to learn from the others and from the situation is a good thing. The wish to learn will ease the situation and help us not to take misunderstandings personally. If one of the others says something which seems strange or highly inappropriate, we can control our feelings and avoid reacting impulsively. Take a quick mental step back, look at the situation from above, and ask yourself "Why am I about to get cross?" "It's very interesting that he should say that." "What's happening?" "What makes him say that?" "How could this be understood differently from the way I heard it?"

When we're together with people who think and act differently from ourselves, we must be able to tolerate being in a situation of uncertainty, where it is unclear what norms and rules apply, and where reactions and next moves cannot be predicted. An important part of the intercultural engagement is therefore to be fully present and attentive during a cross-cultural encounter. To be present is to focus one's attention on the situation. It is to be in contact with the other person, but also with oneself in order to register one's own reactions. It is necessary to be fully present and to listen attentively in order to discover the silences, shifts in atmosphere and other small signs in oneself and the other party which indicate that we need to work to communicate better. To be attentive and present can create the mental 'link' through to the other party.

2. Cultural understanding

Cultural understanding is the knowledge and mental dimension of cultural intelligence. Cultural understanding is both about having an understanding of one's own culture, and being able to understand people with another cultural base when they are facing us in the cross-cultural encounter. This requires a general knowledge of what culture is, and of the role cultural differences play in the meeting of different cultures.

To have a cultural self-perception is to see yourself as a cultural being, and to recognise that some of the things you do are culturally determined, and not the only right or possible thing to do. It is also to be aware that we ourselves also play a part in what happens in the meeting of cultures because such a meeting is the interplay between two parties who think and act differently. It is about taking a step back and trying to look at yourself from the outside. An example of a project of cultural understanding of self is provided by a Danish local authority, which undertook a major project in 2003–

2005 aimed at attracting, integrating and keeping employees with a background other than Danish. Instead of teaching people about 'foreign cultures', the main activity was short 'reversed culture courses', where all ethnic Danes were asked to explore their Danish workplace culture. The participants were able to see themselves as cultural beings and to learn something about the role of culture in the workplace. This process resulted in a more open culture in the organisation, and the employees became better at cooperating with each other and with people from other cultures.

We can learn to understand another person by having a general knowledge of cultural differences and from specific knowledge of the other person's culture. General knowledge creates awareness of the existence of other cultures where people act in ways that are different from our own, and of the fact that their way can be just as right or sensible as one's own. Specific knowledge creates an awareness of features of the other culture which are different from those of one's own. If not warned in advance, Scandinavians will, when asked for lunch for the first time by French business connections, quietly wonder at being sat down to a multi-course meal with wine which takes a couple of hours of the expensive meeting time. But with a knowledge of French business culture, they will be aware that these hours may well be the most productive part of the day, as this is where the opportunity arises for different types of conversations and for 'creative short circuiting' of the formal problem-solving process.

Cultural understanding implies an understanding of the situation; that is, the ability to sense and discover that cultural differences are at play, and to find out how best to manoeuvre in the situation. It is useful to train your eye to discover all the tiny signals and signs at micro-level, and your understanding that others may attach a different and greater importance to them than you. We all use our eyes for small signals when, for example, we are invited to a formal dinner and find ourselves placed at the high table with the VIPs, and we don't know the rules of behaviour for such events. Our attention immediately intensifies in an attempt to watch what the others are doing and when they are doing it, in order to quickly adjust our own actions and not make a fool of ourselves.

If, however, the event is not a once-only dinner invitation but the introduction to a new family-in-law whose culture is highly different from our own, it is not enough merely to ape the others intelligently by watching the micro-level signals. To understand the new culture and get along with it in the long term, we must discover the patterns underlying the details and the significance attached to rituals and jargon.

Cultural understanding is also about distilling experience from cultural encounters in one cultural field and transforming them into general knowledge of cultural mechanisms, that is asking ourselves the questions "What's happening here?" "What mechanisms are at play?" "What was my share in this?" "What other interpretations of the situation could be relevant?"

Having appointed a number of people with differing ethnic backgrounds, a company set to work on ethnic diversity. One of the main points in this work was to look at each other's competences and not at colour and other differences. Shortly after this, the company merged with another company and the human resources development manager now used the same points about integration of differences and building bridges between them. "As you know, we've just seen how well it works to focus on competences instead of differences. This is what we now have to do again in order to integrate with the other company." The cultural mechanisms at play are comparable whether we speak of vocational, ethnic, national or organisational cultural differences, and we gain in insight as we combine understandings across all fields.

Cultural understanding provides a framework for understanding which can prepare us for all sorts of cultural encounters, and it equips us with the mental preparedness to understand what is going on and to let us place our own cultural understanding of self on hold for a short while. It gives flexibility, and thus allows us to see what happens in cultural encounters from several angles, and to be prepared for the encounter so that a different response from the one expected will not take us by surprise. It also allows us to look at the situation in a broader perspective and not to exaggerate the importance of cultural differences.

3. Intercultural communication

Intercultural communication is the action dimension of cultural intelligence, and the name is based on a broad understanding of communication. It involves verbal and non-verbal communication as well as written and possibly other means of expression. It is impossible not to communicate, as passivity and silence are also types of communication which will be noted and interpreted by our surroundings.

Intercultural communication is about the practical aspects of culture; that is, everything that the people at a cross-cultural meeting do in different ways. It is the intercultural communication which brings the other two dimensions of cultural intelligence into the cultural encounter and creates contact between the parties. Cultural understanding which is not brought into play, or intercultural engagement which is not demonstrated, does not create results but remains unfulfilled. It is not an act of cultural intelligence solely to be present with a friendly open attitude and to make yourself available to the other party.

The condition for being able to act appropriately in cultural encounters is the ability to turn off your cultural autopilot and move on to manual control, just as the two dancing partners did. It is necessary to think before speaking and to use more cautious terms than usual – to feel your way and make an effort to understand what the other person is trying to express. We must be able to hold back any impulsive reaction, and change or moderate our expressions. An engineer, for example, will normally react strongly when, in his opinion, another engineer talks nonsense about load-bearing constructions. But when an economist colleague talks the same 'nonsense', the engineer's reaction is much more moderate and the misunderstandings cleared away without any increase in blood pressure.

Changing to manual control does not mean acting a part to 'please' the other party. It is about stopping some of our own cultural routines, habitual expressions and reactions for a while in order to build better contacts with the other party on common ground, where both parties can together find ways to make themselves understood by each other. Both parties are still themselves and authentic persons, like the two dancing partners who finally found a common pattern of movement which became a new dance for the occasion.

It is not always enough for one party to turn to manual control in the cultural encounter. Culturally intelligent communication implies that one can change the discussion to make the participants aware of the situation and enable them to look at it from above. It is a shift to meta-level which means talking about how we talk. As the manager said at the employees' meeting: "In the last hour we have talked about the differences between our two departments and what will be difficult when we merge. What about changing focus and talking about how the two departments resemble each other? If we could calculate the differences, it may be only 10–20 per cent of our work routines which are different." Taking time out in the situation and shifting to meta-level enables us to look at patterns in the discussion and find out how to continue. It helps the participants to turn off the autopilot, and they can then discuss what kind of manual control will be necessary in order to continue.

Culturally intelligent communication means being able to let go of your cultural reservations, cross a threshold of embarrassment, and deliberately try out a question or an action. It is about taking an initiative and reacting when something unexpected happens. It is about handling your own cultural routines in the situation, observing yourself and adjusting your present actions to make them more appropriate. Otherwise the issue must be reopened at the next encounter.

It is important to have the courage to experiment and take a new approach to the situation, to feel your way and find 'new steps' in intercultural communication.

A Norwegian company had a Turkish partner on whose supplies the Norwegian company was very dependent. Things did not go well at the start, as the Turkish partner delivered too little too late, although the Norwegian negotiators had expressly asked the Turkish manager whether his company would be able to deliver the quantities on the deadlines proposed, and had received a positive answer every time. The problem was only solved when the Norwegians realised that the Turkish manager did not like to say no. Then they found different ways of asking and making agreements. They would, for example, turn the question around from asking "Can you deliver this quantity on that date?" to "Is this too much for you?" Things also improved when they spent more time on their visits to the factory and spoke of other things as well as business.

Persistence is important in cultural encounters. We should not give up at the first hurdle or unexpected response. It is necessary to keep a steady gaze on the possibilities in the situation and not be distracted by all the limitations or impossibilities. It's important to press on a little, and perhaps test different kinds of action in order to improve contact. It is also important to ask for feedback from the others in the situation in order to balance our own angles and adjust our own actions.

The action dimension comprises aspects of body and space as well as physical movement. Sometimes, intercultural communication can be about planning the physical venue for cross-cultural meetings in a manner that makes all parties feel comfortable and at home. Many feelings and status signals may be present in the choice of room, space and distribution, and it is important that the physical framework supports the intention of the cultural encounter.

Three local authorities were to merge. One consequence was that the staff from the two small units were to move into the premises of the big unit's administration. The director wanted to avoid a situation in which the new colleagues would feel like outsiders, and he wanted to promote a feeling that everybody was now about to build up a new administration unit together. It was therefore agreed that all staff were to move into a new office so that it was not only those from 'outside' who had to move. It meant more mess and more moving, but it created a common atmosphere of "Now we'll all start something new together."

In order to communicate in a culturally appropriate manner in all of these ways, it is necessary to have a store of communicative forms and methods for improving contact ready for action at the cultural encounter. One must be able to transfer experiences gained in one cultural field to another, as combining one's methods from different fields creates more scope for action. One must know ways of relaxing and de-escalating a situation and ways of talking at meta-level. One must know how to move a discussion from the emotional to the professional level when necessary – and vice versa. One must be able to enter into dialogue about different values. It can also be useful to be able to gain inspiration from another cultural field if caught up in misunderstandings and emotional reactions.

The three dimensions of cultural intelligence in mutual interplay

The tripartite division of the heading above is intended as a model for recognising and improving various types of cultural encounters in the world of business and at the workplace. Intercultural engagement, cultural understanding and intercultural communication are three different aspects of cultural intelligence, and it is important to be able to separate them. The logic of feelings is different from the logic of actions, which in turn differs from the logic of the rational understanding, but at the same time they are all related to each other as domains of cultural interactions. CI is the overarching system in which the three dimensions are embedded sub-systems.

At the same time, cultural intelligence is a dynamic unity of the three dimensions, and none of the three dimensions can stand alone or be understood in isolation. We do not become culturally intelligent by having a good cultural understanding of ourselves and a considerable knowledge of other cultures if we cannot contain our own and other people's emotional reactions, and lack the courage to take initiatives in a cultural encounter. We cannot be highly motivated to build bridges to other cultures, and courageous in relation to testing various types of dialogue, unless we also have a cultural understanding of ourselves and a knowledge of the kinds of cultural factors which may be at play.

In practical terms, intercultural engagement, cultural understanding and intercultural communication are closely intertwined in cultural encounters, as they influence each other mutually. They can confirm each other and strengthen each other, and they can disrupt and jostle each other. They can turn into negative cycles creating negative dynamics by increasing misunderstandings, thus increasing the distance between people, or they can turn into positive cycles, creating positive dynamics with learning and mutual understanding, and we call this latter process the development of cultural intelligence.

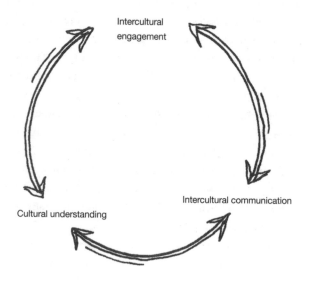

Intercultural engagement

Intercultural communication

Cultural understanding

Cultural intelligence is something which individuals have and apply, but we believe that it also gives meaning to use the CI concept in relation to groups and organisations. For example, the level of cultural intelligence in a group or organisation can be determined by looking at:

- How different cultures are spoken about and how they are handled both internally and in relation to external partners.
- The attitudes and understandings of culture and cultural differences which exist among management and employees.
- What cultural differences are represented where, how they are utilised, and for what.
- Whether there are cultural differences within management.
- How procedures and work routines are organised in relation to creating scope for members to learn from each other's cultures, and confronting them to promote new thinking.
- The relationships which exist between power differences and cultural differences.
- How much is invested in the development of cultural intelligence.

A negative circle

It is not difficult to imagine a self-fuelling vicious circle once two colleagues get off course, and the two have mentally stepped on each other's toes. An example is provided by a merger where one employee from the big company and one from the small company left a meeting in one of the preparatory working groups feeling nettled, each with his own version of what had taken place. We'll call the two companies Big-tec and Small-tec.

In brief, the situation was that the two merging companies were to exchange experiences about a procedure, but the meeting developed into long explanations by the Big-tec employee, while his colleague from Small-tec mainly kept silent. Each had brought an understanding of his own culture and a perception of the other party's culture with them to the meeting. Big-tec were proud of being among the biggest in the industry and were looking forward to becoming even bigger. They described Big-tec's culture as being professional and focused on individual competences. Their preconception of Small-tec was that it was probably no coincidence that they hadn't grown any bigger, and that they seemed to have rather a family culture, where tasks were distributed according to who knew whom. Small-tec were proud of their informal and creative approach, and they saw their own culture as human and flexible. They saw Big-tec as bureaucratic and hierarchical, where people where highly preoccupied with rules and titles.

After the meeting, they had the following interpretations of what had taken place: Small-tec employee: "It's OK that the fellow from Big-tec started by telling us about their experience. They're more used to big systems than we are of course. But he just kept talking on and on, and when I asked about something, he simply brushed it aside. I found that very unpleasant. To tell the truth, I was really peeved. I got the impression that he thought his system so excellent that it would of course be introduced without change into our new common business. He had no interest at all in my experience, so he didn't get to hear about it. I simply pulled in my horns. How did he come across to me? Self-important bordering on megalomaniac."

Big-tec employee: "I was asked to start by presenting our experience, but the fellow from Small-tec kept interrupting me with critical questions. I don't think they liked being the small partner in this merger, and he gave the impression that he was constantly on guard. That was until he packed up entirely and never said a word. I wonder if he really understands what a system of this size must be able to handle? I certainly had the impression that all of a sudden, he had nothing to offer. It will be annoying if I have to do all the hard work in this working group."

Why did the meeting fail? Was it Small-tec's first question? Or was it Big-tec seeing the question as critical? Was it that they had excessively strong preconceptions of each other, or was it simply misunderstandings which arose during the situation itself? It is pointless to discuss whose fault it was, as both parties had a share in the tit-for-tat which followed, and which prevented the building of a good dialogue about the professional goal. It is not possible to point to any one problematic move on which to blame the vicious circle.

Let us look at the example in light of the three dimensions, using the abbreviations ICE (intercultural engagement), CU (cultural understanding) and ICC (intercultural communication):

- Both parties had a low level of preparedness and paid no attention to the fact that different cultures were present (CU). This influenced their actions (ICC), as they were still on autopilot and were unwittingly acting on their own cultural repertoire as if they were among colleagues at home in the company.
- Both parties had a stereotypical home-grown view of each other's culture and motives (CU). This meant that the other party's actions were interpreted in light of their preconceived views, thus confirming their own cultural viewpoints (CU).
- The party who withdrew into his shell, omitting to act and ask

(ICC), lost the opportunity to check his personal understanding and amend his personal interpretations (CU) of the other party's actions. This meant that he continued to take cultural misunderstandings personally (ICE). To do so blocks contact and lessens the motivation to clear up cultural misunderstandings and improve the situation (ICE).

- The inability to control their own cultural emotional routine reaction (ICE) will have been expressed in their body language (ICC), and the negative feelings reduced their interest in seeking a better cultural understanding of the other party (CU).

If a misunderstanding has been taken as a personal affront with the result that the parties have offended each other, they will need the help of a third person. This is because taking offence is like putting on blinkers. The people involved will be unable to understand or act because they are unable to ignore their own reactions and move the dialogue into the professional field. Their understanding of and interest in the other party has disappeared, and so has their motivation for salvaging the situation.

Cultural intelligence in all its three dimensions was thus lacking from Small-tec and Big-tec at the meeting of the two parties, and the contact between them unfortunately became worse as the meeting went on. This of course meant that the professional work of exchanging experiences and finding a shared solution suffered.

A positive circle

In order to develop a high level of cultural intelligence, all three dimensions must influence each other in a positive self-reinforcing circle. Surely we all remember instances where we succeeded in building new cooperative relations with a person who was different from ourselves – how an initial hesitant contact increased interest in getting to know each other better, and how questions from unexpected angles opened the door to a dialogue on each other's different experiences – how better understanding led to greater trust, and so on. Sometimes the process is easy, while at other times it is more of a challenge and requires more effort.

By using our cultural intelligence, we are able to establish common ground at a cultural encounter: "We agree on this point and here we can meet." If we focus on all the differences, we increase the mental distance, and things can become very complicated and difficult to tackle. The most important point is therefore to reduce the complexity of the situation and find something on which the parties agree. However many cultural differences, there will also be some points of similarity between the parties and probably a shared purpose for meeting. Focusing on this can reduce the distance and increase the trust between the parties, and thus enable them to find and express their points of similarity and common features. Shared goals must be discussed in depth to ensure that everybody has the same understanding of the words used. It is possible to reduce the complexity of communicating and create a common culture by agreeing on ground rules for the partnership, including, for example, the manner of dialogue and handling of disagreements.

A consultancy firm had established a working group to survey the Swedish and the French markets before launching a new product. After an initial meeting in which the Swedish and French members of the group had met each other and agreed on methods and deadlines for the various phases of the survey, the group conferred largely via telephone conferences between the two countries. Some small misunderstandings arose early in the process. The main one was that the French and the Swedish members had different perceptions of what a deadline means. When the deadline was up for part of the survey, the Swedes sat ready with the agreed materials, whereas the French had very good explanations as to why it had been more important to spend time on another aspect of the survey, so they hadn't been able to finish on time. The Swedes thought their French colleagues sloppy and unreliable, and the French found the Swedes rigid in not wanting to deviate from a plan even if there was good reason for doing so. After a discussion, the expression 'southern flexibility' was coined for the French participants' attitude to deadlines, and this expression improved the mutual understanding and generated a disarming humour. What had been a problem in the partnership was given a name, and that helped when deadlines were agreed.

Common ground is the information, knowledge and beliefs which a group has in common, and their awareness that the group has this information and knowledge in common, as the American organisation experts Olson and Olson put it. Common ground clears the path to trust, where the parties gain the courage to interact in the somewhat insecure context of a cultural encounter. Small and big markers of the common ground will create a common culture in the situation, and gradually, the parties will build a knowledge of one another and experiences in understanding each other. Common ground is the base and the launching pad, and the parties can return to it and seek clarity if misunderstandings should arise, and thus continue to build their common culture.

Cultural intelligence is more than tolerance

Cultural intelligence qualifies cultural encounters and creates greater intercultural understanding across vocational, national, ethnic, and organisational divides. To this should be added that cultural intelligence offers a new strategy in situations where communication may be hampered or marked by mutual stereotyping. Such situations may arise in workplaces where employees who are different from the majority are discriminated against, or find that they are being treated with reserve, perhaps because their colleagues are afraid of discriminating against them or of crossing one of their personal boundaries.

If we consider the ordinary social life of a workplace, it may happen that homosexuals, elderly colleagues, immigrants or women in men's jobs experience an unpleasant kind of attention from their colleagues, making them feel different and not entirely part of the workplace community. It is unpleasant to be 'singled out' and treated as a representative of a whole group, as the only male employee in the company's accounts department learned when asked the following question across the lunch table after a week of many media reports on rape and sexual harassment: "Why don't men understand a No?"

It may be fine to seek to have your curiosity satisfied face to face with a colleague who is different from you. It can become a dialogue between equal partners where both partners learn something new, provided the two know each other, and that the curiosity is genuine and matched by a willingness to talk about oneself. But if the same curious questions are asked in the presence of others, the effect will be quite different. A personal contact is established in the former situation, while the latter situation is about generalisations, about a negative labelling of a person, and about invasion of personal space. It is the opposite of culturally intelligent behaviour.

It is not enough to be tolerant of each other's differences in the sense of letting each other be. This would be a lack of respect, and an avoidance of contact about something important in order to ensure that you can go on thinking of yourself as the more sensible and right-minded person. Genuine respect for a person from another culture than your own requires entering into dialogue about each other's different values and attitudes.

> A Danish company had found a new group leader in a technical field, but the group members went to management to complain about its choice. They did not want a female group leader because "We cannot respect a female leader." They were all men, and most came from a Middle Eastern background. Management then appointed a male group leader instead in the belief that the group's resistance was too strong for it to work with a female leader. Management may have thought that they were showing tolerance towards the men whose cultural background gave them a view of male and female roles which was different from the Danish view, but the culturally intelligent thing to have done would have been to initiate a discussion with the workers about each other's values and views of women and men. The company would then have been able to insist that leaders were appointed on the basis of qualifications, that the company stood for certain values, and that it was fine for the workers to have different values as long as this had no influence on the professional life of the workplace.

In the course of normal social interaction at the workplace, individuals may experience different pauses in communication around them. It may be that certain topics of conversation are avoided, or that silence suddenly falls, or a brief hesitation is felt. This creates distance between the people involved, even where the intention is friendly and caring. The colleagues may be afraid of offending the person by saying the wrong thing relative to the non-discrimination rules. It is understandable if such awkward pauses in communication occur when a new and different colleague has just been appointed; but if this pattern continues after the parties have got to know each other, misunderstandings can arise, along with mistrust and exclusion from the social life of the workplace, and the effect of this will be felt both on the working environment and the results. Cultural intelligence is about creating the best possible contact among people across cultural divides, and in some cases especially about demystifying the topics that are avoided, developing skills in talking about difficult issues, and inspiring ground rules which will generate closer contacts.

Cultural intelligence in relation to other broad concepts of intelligence

We now turn to compare cultural intelligence with other concepts and theories of intelligence. Our concept of cultural intelligence belongs to the same tradition as the American psychologist David Goleman's concepts of emotional intelligence (EQ) and social intelligence (SQ). This tradition is different from the school of thought which reserves the word 'intelligence' for the ability to learn. Our interest is to pinpoint intelligent practice in the many situations in everyday working life where culture plays an important role, and this includes knowledge and skills as well as the ability to learn. Whereas classical intelligence theories link intelligence (IQ) to individual and partially genetically determined resources, our concept refers to a practice and a potential for development in a person, a group or a company.

The broad concept of intelligence gained significant ground in 1983 with Howard Gardner's book *Frames of Mind. The Theory of Multiple Intelligences*. Gardner's research showed that human intelligence was not a single cognitive dimension measured in IQ, but rather a combination of abilities described in seven categories of intelligence: linguistic, logical–mathematical, spatial, bodily/kinaesthetic, musical, interpersonal and intrapersonal.

In 1990, American psychologists Peter Salovey and John Mayer proposed a theory of emotional intelligence (intrapersonal intelligence, according to Gardner's theory), and in 1992, the American–Israeli psychologist Reuven Bar-On wrote a doctoral thesis on the topic. Daniel Goleman popularised these theories under the term 'emotional intelligence' (EQ), taking inspiration from more recent brain research into the irrational aspects of the psyche. Goleman's concept represents a breakthrough in the work of demonstrating how important emotional competences are for people's ability to lead, cooperate and achieve results in today's workplaces.

In Goleman's version (Goleman, 1998), emotional intelligence (EQ) includes:

Self-awareness: the ability to be aware of our emotions at any given moment and to use these preferences to guide our decisions. It is also having a realistic assessment of our own abilities and being in possession of a sound and solid feeling of self-confidence – our inner compass.

Self-management: the ability to harness our moods and feelings to prevent them from standing in the way of the task in hand, and to lighten it instead. It is also being conscientious and putting off gratifying our desires in order to reach our goals. And finally, it is being good at putting emotional discomfort behind ourselves – self-control.

Self-motivation: the ability to use our strongest preferences to move and steer ourselves towards our goal. Motivation also helps us to take initiatives and improve ourselves, as well as to be persistent in the face of obstacles and frustration – it is what moves us.

Social awareness: the ability to recognise and understand what other people feel, to be able to look at things from other people's perspectives, and to maintain friendships and keep social relations with many different people – our social antennae.

Relationship management: the ability to harness emotions in relation to others and to be able to read social situations and networks accurately. It is also the ability to get along with others without friction and to use these skills to persuade, lead, negotiate and settle disagreements and inspire cooperation and teamwork – the art of influencing.

The sister concept of social intelligence (SQ) began to appear later in books on management. The concept was first used in 1920 by the American psychologist Edward Thorndike, but it has only gained popularity in recent years. Several writers have published books on social intelligence in the period from 2002 to 2006, but it will probably be Daniel Goleman's definition of the concept from autumn 2006 which will come to dominate. Goleman takes his starting point in Gardner's seven intelligences, which are about the processes which take place between people, and his concept of social intelligence is based on the discovery from brain research of the so-called 'mirror neurons' which scientists believe are the biological explanation of our ability to empathise with other people.

Goleman divides SQ into social awareness and social skills. Social awareness is what we are sensible of in others, and the concept covers the entire spectrum from a momentary recognition of another person's mood to awareness of complicated social situations. Social awareness comprises the following abilities:

Primary empathy: the ability to feel for others, to read other people's non-verbal emotional signals, even when they believe that they are hiding what they feel.

Synchrony: the ability to listen with your full attention and to focus on the other person, to step into another person's shoes and understand the other person's needs and motives.

Empathic precision: the ability to understand another person's thoughts, feelings and intentions – a conscious awareness of the other person's motives.

Social awareness: the ability to know how the social world functions and being able to interpret social situations which are the basis of how well we manage in a social context.

Social skills are what we use our social awareness for, and they comprise the following aspects:

Synchrony: the ability to enter into frictionless non-verbal interaction, the ability to get on to the same wavelength as another person, including by acting on non-verbal signals.

Self-presentation: the ability to present yourself with effect. This includes the ability to time yourself, to control your emotions, and to attune yourself to the situation.

Influence: the ability to generate results from social interactions in a constructive manner, to act with social presence of mind so as not to create unnecessary disturbance.

Participation: the ability to show concern for the needs of others and sympathy for their situation in practical terms, to be able to assist and generate group cooperation around a common goal.

Cultural intelligence in relation to emotional and social intelligence

Emotional intelligence (EQ) is an intrapersonal intelligence, although Goleman also coupled it with a social dimension, and social intelligence (SQ) is an interpersonal intelligence. In this book, the term 'cultural intelligence' includes both the interpersonal and intrapersonal aspects. Cultural intelligence is more, however, than the sum of the two. It is a special form of intelligence which extends beyond the boundaries of both emotional and social intelligence.

The point of cultural intelligence is that both emotional reactions and human relations are culturally determined. The aspect of social intelligence which concerns the reading of non-verbal emotional signals will, for example, change character when observed across cultures, with different norms for how and when it is appropriate to express your emotions, and to whom they can be expressed. The norms differ from the blacksmith to the executive suite to kindergarten teachers, and so they do from east to west and north to south throughout the world.

Another aspect of social intelligence, the ability to present yourself effectively, must also be viewed in a cultural context. Being 'honest and frank' does, for example, carry different meanings in different cultures. A comment which in one company will be seen in positive terms as honest and frank will be felt in another organisation to be brutal and undiplomatic, and hence negative. 'Honest and frank' will also mean something different to a Danish and to a Japanese person. In Denmark it is a virtue, while in Japan, not losing face is more important than being honest. So when people communicate across cultural divides, it is not enough to have emotional and social intelligence. Cultural intelligence is also required for the result to be successful.

The three CI dimensions intercultural engagement, cultural understanding and intercultural communication have several points in common with Goleman's emotional and social intelligence. Goleman's components of emotional intelligence – self-awareness, self-management, motivation and empathy – are similar to intercultural engagement and cultural understanding in many ways, and some of the aspects of social intelligence can be recognised in cultural intelligence, but with the important difference that cultural intelligence proceeds across cultural differences, and therefore requires some additional competences.

Cultural intelligence requires a global awareness of the surrounding world and the ability to act in complex situations. The situation in a cultural encounter is not one-dimensional, but multi-dimensional, and if misunderstandings occur, the situation must be assessed from several angles: "Is this about our different educational backgrounds?" "Is this because my ethnic background is different from his?" "Is this because we come from different companies?" It is necessary to be aware of the many perceptions present and to try to clear a path into dialogue at a relevant point. If misunderstandings are reduced to a personal issue between two parties, it is difficult to establish common ground and learn from the situation.

Cultural intelligence provides us with methods of interpretation and a range of possible actions when people from different cultural backgrounds meet. Cultural intelligence also comprises several elements which are not present in emotional or social intelligence. They include cultural translation of the reactions of self and others, a learning attitude towards cultural differences, cultural self-awareness, and a knowledge of culture and its role in communication. One forms the impression that Goleman developed the two forms of intelligence on the basis of the North American and western European cultures.

CI should not be confused with CQ

There are various cultural intelligence concepts with different focus and content. The phrase 'Cultural Intelligence' was introduced in an article in the United States in 2002 by the international management expert P. Christopher Earley, and he published the first book on cultural intelligence with Soon Ang in the following year. Their book was soon followed by publications by other writers, but we follow Earley, Ang and Tan's (2006) use of the concept as the other writers appear to be staying within the same framework, and they all abbreviate their cultural intelligence concepts 'CQ'.

CQ is based on the descriptive cultural understanding which sees culture as something we have inside us which governs our actions, and which can therefore be used to predict and explain people's thoughts and reactions. CQ is defined as a person's ability to adapt successfully to new cultural surroundings, and it is used predominantly about national cultures. It is mainly about a person's ability to adapt to social and working life in a foreign country, but it can also be used about a person's ability to lead a multi-national group. Earley and Ang see national culture as our primary culture, while a person's other cultural identities are seen as subcultures of the national culture. We do not share this view. Our definition of cultural intelligence is based on the understanding of culture as a process – a point we return to in the next chapter.

This book's concept of cultural intelligence owes its name to inspiration from the American concept, and so does the tripartite division of the concept into "mind, heart and muscle"; but our version of the three dimensions is different because the focus and the content of the two concepts are different. We have chosen the abbreviation 'CI' for our version of cultural intelligence to indicate that it differs from a quotient such as IQ. In schematic form, the most important differences between the two concepts are:

Differences between CQ and CI

	Earley, Ang and Tan's concept (CQ)	This book's concept (CI)
Understanding of culture (see Chapter 2)	Descriptive concept (culture as an essence)	The complex concept (culture as a process)
Purpose of using one's intelligence	That a person may cope well in a new culture	To act appropriately in cultural encounters and contribute to better mutual understanding
Goal	Overcoming barriers between cultures	To generate a shared bridge-building culture between several cultures (with focus on both differences and similarities between several cultures)
Focus	Predominantly national cultures	All kinds of cultural identities
Who can have this intelligence?	Individuals	Individuals, groups and organisations
View of human nature/psychological theory	People's views and reactions can be predicted	People's views and reactions must be experienced and explored in the situation

The culturally intelligent person in a cultural encounter	A skilled actor who imitates the person from the other culture	Is himself, but can turn off his own cultural autopilot (see Chapter 2)
Development and use of cultural intelligence	CQ can be measured by a test	CI is assessed while it is being developed

According to the theory of CQ, we can measure our level of cultural intelligence by choosing self-descriptions in a test, such as: "When I'm in a different cultural situation, I can feel immediately if things are going well or if something is wrong." Or "I can easily change my behaviour when this is required in an intercultural situation." But in our view, such self-descriptive tests make no sense, because we are often not aware of our own actions and interpretations as manifestations of culture, and we can easily have numerous blind spots. We may well find ourselves in a situation where we are not aware of all the cultural differences present in the group. If we do not then receive a direct response, we will leave the meeting believing that our behaviour was appropriate, while other members of the group may well conclude that we acted disrespectfully or otherwise inappropriately. It is difficult to see yourself from the outside. We see our surroundings through our cultural glasses, and this makes it impossible for us to seriously assess our own level of cultural intelligence.

When we apply our understanding of culture and cultural intelligence, it makes sense to assess the level of cultural intelligence via dialogue and processes with other participants; and to do so will simultaneously develop the participants' cultural intelligence. We will return to this point in the final chapter, but first we need to look more closely at what culture is, its importance, and why it matters which definition of culture we use.

2/

WHAT IS CULTURE?

Culture is like a tailwind on a bicycle path. We don't notice it until we change direction and find it going against us

Culture and cultural differences are important in more work situations than one would automatically think. There are cultural differences between merging organisations and between enterprises entering into new strategic alliances. There are cultural differences between staff in the finance department and staff in R&D, as there are between colleagues of Danish and of Middle Eastern origin. There are cultural differences between the American parent company and the German subsidiary, and between the Norwegian manager and his staff in the French branch. Culture and cultural differences affect our way of thinking and acting, and therefore also the results we achieve, and whether we achieve them.

A professional approach to cultural differences can be a gold mine for an organisation; and vice versa, a problematic cultural encounter can generate misunderstandings and communication breakdowns often leading to less positive results. It is therefore important for business leaders to be familiar with the dynamics of cultural encounters in order for them to handle challenging encounters and to promote constructive relations among different cultures.

In this chapter, we discuss what culture is, what impact it has in different contexts, how it arises, and what happens when people of different cultural backgrounds meet. We examine communication across cultural differences, and finally we analyse what happens when the importance of culture is either exaggerated or ignored. We take a broad approach to culture, using examples of cultural features and differences from various areas by way of introducing the next three chapters in which three cultural fields, namely professional, organisational and national cultures, are explored.

Culture is defined in hundreds of different ways. This is because culture is a concept of multiple meanings. It can be viewed from many different angles and used in many different ways. However, it is not culture as an abstract concept which interests us here, but the way in which people understand culture. When and how can the word 'culture' be used to explain something? What importance is placed on culture? What role do culture and cultural differences play in communicating and working together?

This book defines culture as a practice shared by people within a community. Culture is the filter through which we interpret our existence and orient ourselves in order to direct our actions. For members of a community, any cultural context signals a non-verbalised rule for what is right and wrong to do and say in different situations, and triggers in them routines and congenial ways of acting. Our own culture is something which makes us feel at home in our place of work, in our country, in our family, among colleagues of the same profession, and in our ethnic groups. Culture is what we say and do together with other people in ways which distinguish us from other groups and which signals membership of the group. When we are within our own cultural community, culture is a backdrop which we take for granted and do not think about.

Culture is not a thing, but a community which is generated and maintained, and which is subject to gradual change in response to our mutual communication. It is, as the Norwegian organisation consultant Stein Kleppestø puts it, "a group's continuous attempts at defining itself and its situation in order to create meaning out of what happens". Culture is created and changed in a living process as a result of the various contributions of its members. This means that culture is socially constructed.

This book uses a broad concept of culture which extends across a number of different cultural fields. Normally, national cultures are seen as one thing and organisational cultures as something completely different, while differences between trades/professions are hardly even seen as cultural differences. This book stresses the point that cultures, and relations between various cultures, follow the same dynamics and processes, whether we are talking of organisational cultures, national cultures or professional cultures. The same applies to cultural communities based on for example age, gender, social class or sport, but these will not be considered in this book. Within individual cultures and between cultures, there are psychological dynamics and social patterns which influence how people create their identities and function together with others – and thus how they collaborate and perform in the workplace.

When misunderstandings arise between people of different nationalities, it will often be explained with reference to the cultural differences between them, because it is so obvious that they speak different languages, perhaps dress differently, and have different body languages and ways of greeting and talking together. But when misunderstandings occur between different professional groups or people with different organisational attachments within the same organisation, the problem is generally explained as a clash of interests or as a personality conflict. In this case there are no language barriers, and the 'warring parties' are members of the same general corporate culture, so they have many traits in common. Nevertheless, cultural differences may well lie behind their problems, but can go undetected because there is less focus on professional or organisational cultural differences and the complex mix between cultures.

The two dimensions of culture

Culture has two dimensions no matter what cultural field we focus on, and it is necessary to look at both in order to understand a given culture:

Practice: the manifestations of culture which can be seen or heard, for example words, gestures, professional jargon, rituals, working methods, forms of greeting, body language, stories told, or forms of communication. Both language and physical codes are involved.

Forms of understanding: the thoughts and feelings associated with practice and which are often formulated as explanations of the ways things are done in certain situations. They also include self-perception, preconceptions and norms which guide behaviour and carry with them feelings of right and wrong – what we call 'preferences' and what others may call 'values'.

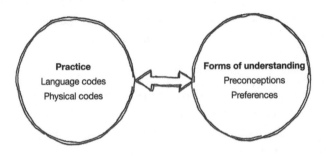

Forms of understanding and practice affect each other, but there is no direct link between a form of practice and a form of understanding. Some forms of understanding are conscious while others are subconscious, but it is possible to make an effort to put words to them and to become conscious of at least some of them.

Self-perception is understanding of oneself, while preconceptions are the opinions we hold of some phenomenon until we learn more. They are oversimplified opinions about people who are different from ourselves, and of whom we have only a limited personal knowledge. This is because preconceptions are based on something we have heard or read, and which may be either right or wrong. Preconceptions generate expectations regarding other people and their reactions. To have preconceptions is neither a positive nor a negative thing. The more aware we become that we have preconceptions, the better will we be able to keep an explorative and open mind, and thus allow our preconceptions to be modified by experience. The two dimensions of culture will be discussed in more detail in Chapter 5, where we focus on national cultural differences.

A much-quoted American organisation specialist, Edgar Schein, operates with a division of culture into artefacts, espoused beliefs and core assumptions. Schein builds on an understanding of culture which is different from ours, but one can say in slightly simplified terms that we have reduced his three levels to two.

Two understandings of culture

There are two basically different ways in which to look at culture. We call one the descriptive understanding and the other the complex understanding. As noted, it is the complex understanding of culture which is used in this book.

The descriptive understanding of culture stems from a traditional view of culture which assumes that people possess a personal core, an essence or an immutable inner nature. This perception is therefore also known as the essentialist view of culture. According to this view, a person's culture determines his or her actions, and it is assumed that any representative of a given cultural group will express the relevant cultural features. Culture is seen as independent of context, and no attention is paid to differences within the culture. Culture is seen as a group's stable system of norms and judgments, and focus is on harmony and uniqueness of reference.

According to this view, culture governs people's actions, and it follows that the manifestations and effects of culture are predictable. Cultural differences are seen as barriers to communication, and culture as an explanation as to why people behave in certain ways. In short, this view sees cause and effect as linearly related. 'Foreign' cultures are described in order to allow us to prepare for encounters with them, and management literature is full of books on how to act and behave in other countries.

The complex understanding of culture sees culture as a practice among people in a community and as a process. The group's culture is a matter for negotiation among its members in different situations, and therefore under constant change. Members express their culture in different ways within the group. The complex view of culture can also be called the constructionist view.

How are we affected by culture?

On our first day in a new workplace, we have a lot of questions about the culture of the place, such as "What should I do to be a good colleague here?" "Should I walk around saying hello to everybody else?" "When and where do I shake hands?" "How should I understand and interpret what the others do?" "Is it OK to ask the boss directly, or should I ask a colleague instead?"

Culture is expressed in our approach to work in the workplace, in body language, management style, ways of greeting, hierarchy, conceptions of time, forms of meeting, dress code, the way the telephone is answered, humour, and so on. Gradually, as we learn to decipher the codes and ground rules of our new workplace and learn to act appropriately, we become full members of the community.

As long as we're within our own culture, we can use our autopilot, as the Norwegian culture expert Øjvind Dahl puts it, because we're moving in a known environment where routines and ways of acting and speaking are ingrained habits. It's easy to make oneself understood to others, and we have no problem understanding what's going on, so without even thinking about it, we turn down our conscious control and allow our bodies to relax into an almost unconscious reflex routine. But as soon as we enter a different culture, the autopilot must be deactivated, and we have to engage manual control and pay more attention, for we are in a situation where we are not quite certain what would be the right or wrong thing to do or say.

Ole had just arrived in the United States for the first time and had to drive a car in Washington. But first, his Danish friend who had lived in the city for a couple of years gave him an initial instruction on how the traffic culture differed from that of Denmark. "Be careful in the big streets. The direction of traffic changes in the middle lane during rush hours, so look up and check for a red cross, which means that it's a one-way lane in the opposite direction. You must be extremely careful not to exceed the speed limits, and there are lots of police on the streets and the fines are high. When you come to a crossing with no lights, people take turns, so check who came first and simply go when it's your turn – otherwise you'll stop the flow through the crossing. You have to give way to cars waiting to get out from side streets". Ole then drove off cautiously, as this could become both a dangerous and expensive experience. His 'autopilot' from the Copenhagen traffic culture had to be totally disconnected, and this was both physically and mentally tiring at the start. It took several days before he dared to enter an empty middle lane for fear of a head-on collision with other cars. Sometimes he forgot to give way to a car entering from a side street and he was sure that they saw him as selfish and rude.

There were clear safety reasons why it was Ole who had to adapt to the American traffic culture in this example, but there are also good reasons for turning to manual control and starting off with caution in personal cultural encounters between equals.

Cultures are something people create by being together, but we don't start from scratch every time. Culture is created on the basis of already-established patterns of action and interpretations of reality. We are born into some cultural communities; others we educate ourselves into; and some we join as members, and this is important for how we acquire the culture and become co-creators of it.

We are born into a family where we absorb and learn our parents' understanding of reality based on factors such as their regional, social and national background. A small child has no possibility of imagining the world differently from the way its parents present it, so for better or worse, everything is taken for granted as the normal way to think, say and do things. Everything else is abnormal and wrong. Only later in life do we (possibly) become aware that we're wearing cultural glasses, and that others are also wearing glasses and experiencing things in other ways. But the culture we're born into is difficult to change, for it has been imprinted on us before we learned to speak, and it is stored in our bodies.

Body language is the body's unconscious form of expression. An example is the different ways in which national cultures experience the distance between two people. When a person from Sweden and a person from Spain have a conversation at a reception, one notices how the Swede is slowly backing away in order to increase the mutual distance, while the Spaniard on his part is moving forward in order to decrease it. The Spaniard experiences 'too great a distance' as a weak contact which may be about to be broken, while the Swede experiences 'too short a distance' as insecurity and a feeling that the other is being pushy. But when the Swede then meets a Japanese, it is the Japanese who will be backing round the room. None of these people has ever been explicitly told that a certain distance between two people is right, but they have learnt it as part of growing up and by copying their surroundings, and by reacting to different signals expressing acceptance or the opposite from other people.

It is easier to become aware of one's professional or workplace culture because we only become members of these as adults, when we already have a pattern of understanding and acting which will differ in some ways from the new culture we are moving into. But once we have adapted ourselves to our profession or workplace, we also take that culture for granted. A cultural membership can thus be like a game where nobody can explain the rules, but everybody knows how to follow them.

We're all part of several cultures

Every person is a member of many different groups, and thus cultures. Each group membership gives us a cultural identity which is generated together with the other people in the group and activated when we identify with that side of ourselves. The British culture expert Stuart Hall works on the concept of 'cultural identities' as aspects of a person's identity which are generated by membership of different cultures. Hall points out that we choose our identity, but that it is created in contact with other people in the manner in which we are spoken to and listened to. A person's cultural identities can be diverse and mutually contradictory without being in any way schizophrenic. Consider, for example, the account of Karen's day:

> Karen is working in a big drug company and is reminded of it every morning when she turns in through the gate displaying the company logo. She feels

she belongs to the place when moving around among her colleagues, and she is proud when told that the newest sales figures show that they have overtaken their biggest competitor. She is a member of the company's building and construction group and she is due to attend a meeting in the morning with the municipal technical administration about the company's plans for an extension. The meeting may remind her of her identity as an employee in the private sector, where the culture is quite different from that in the city administration. She attends a department meeting in the afternoon, where she exercises her identity as leader within the management culture of which she is a part. She is reminded of how it was to be a rank and file worker with less influence, but also with less responsibility for the difficult decisions. When a discussion develops on the type of qualifications which should be required in an appointment to a vacant position, she expresses her opinion as a chemical engineer and not as a biologist or pharmacist. On her way home from work she shops in a DIY centre where she meets only men on her way round the aisles, and she notices that the talk is quite different from what she would hear in a fashion shop for women. Her son has friends visiting and they talk of conflicts and cliques at school, and Karen has a very clear sense of herself – for better or worse – as an adult person who has become better at forgiving herself and others.

Karen's story is equally valid in other relations in life, as a person's identity is formed by numerous memberships and cultural identities. We are all members of several cultures at one and the same time. Our cultures play a different role in different situations, and how we handle and combine the various sides of our identity is entirely individual.

A person's identity is dynamic. It develops and changes depending on the context in which we find ourselves, the impressions we note, and the ways in which we meet other people. Identity is thus a social construct, as it is the situation and the other people we meet that decide which part of our identity we activate. This means that a person *is* not in a certain way, but that she presents herself and is perceived in certain ways. This should not be understood to mean that we are all actors slipping in and out of various roles depending on the situation and whom we meet. We develop our various cultural identities during childhood by comparing ourselves with and differentiating ourselves from parents, siblings and other people of importance to us, and by the influences exerted by school, education and the course of life in general and our own response to our surroundings.

Which of our multiple cultural identities will come to the fore and become important depends on the situation and our interpretation, but some cultural imprints are more dominant than others. A person's national culture is part of our early imprinting and it is constantly reinforced by the media, which play an important role in producing our shared consciousness via its sorting of news and the angle from which it is told. "That is un-Danish..." has become a weighty argument in public debates, and "What should we Danish people think about this?" is a question often raised in the news media. The Danish national self-perception has been activated strongly in the wake of globalisation, and it is being constantly reinforced in public debate. In their annual New Year speeches to the nation, the Queen and the Prime Minister put Danish culture into words and express who they think the Danes are:

It is perhaps typical of us in Denmark that we do not like conflicts; we prefer a discussion to end in agreement between all parties. We find it difficult to take strongly expressed opinions, categorical demands and dramatic statements seriously, and we often react either by sniggering or feeling offended.

The Queen's New Year speech, 31 December 2005

National culture has deeper roots than other cultural identities, but this does not necessarily mean that it is more important to us than other cultural memberships. National culture will, just like other sides of our identity, be important to us in some situations and entirely without importance in others. National identity also plays a different role for different people, in that some people from Norway identify very strongly with being Norwegian, while others are more oriented towards being Europeans or Scandinavians in the world. Moreover, in more recent times it was only when Danish society also began to include people from other national backgrounds that the need to define Danish culture arose. This applies to all cultures: a culture only stands out clearly when confronted with something different.

We sort ourselves and each other

We all seek to order our understanding of our surroundings by sorting and categorising ourselves and others on the basis of group relationships. Much of this process is automatic and unconscious, a fact which we only discover when the mechanism breaks down. Gender is one of the most obvious categories, and it is only when the automatic sorting mechanism cannot distinguish the gender of a person that we suddenly become conscious of the process. We hesitate, look once more and wonder: "Is that a woman or a man?"

The sorting mechanisms change in step with changes in one's own life. As brand-new parents, we are particularly aware of other prams and find it incredible how many people have had a baby at the same time as us. It is the process of perceiving which is playing tricks on us. There are no more prams than usual, but prams have gained a new importance in our lives. A pram is seen as a sign that others are in the same situation, and points out members of the group of parents of small children. "My God, are there really that many of us!"

This example shows that we do not perceive ourselves and our surroundings objectively as through a lens or tape recorder. Some sorting mechanisms are active processes, and part of our perception of ourselves in the contexts we enter into. Other parts of them are less conscious, but sorting always proceeds as a comparison with something else.

It's important to belong

We understand ourselves by making comparisons with others. By categorising ourselves and others, we construct and reinforce our identity. Our image of ourselves is composed of things with which we identify and things from which we distance ourselves – elements we share with others and elements which distinguish us from others. "I'm happy to be Swedish, we don't have such rigid hierarchies in the workplaces – we can talk directly to the boss." "I'm happy I live in a small community where we look after each other, and not in a big city where people can die in their flats without anybody noticing."

It is very important for a person to belong to a culture. It lends meaning to our actions and forms our ways of thinking and acting. It is a general human trait to wish for acceptance and the ability to make ourselves understood, and to make a constructive contribution to results within our community. Membership of a group means to be 'in' and to feel right and normal, and the cultural community lends a group identity and contributes to its members' personal identities via professional jargon, working methods and self-perception. "I'm an HR employee." "I work for Microsoft." "I collect stamps." We place ourselves in society and are placed in society via our group memberships.

All cultures have codes which set them apart from other cultures. Codes are certain forms of language and physical expressions which communicate a certain message in ultra-short form. Every profession has its own technical terms and a language code which carries a precise meaning to members of the profession, but which can be totally obscure to outsiders. The IT world has numerous abbreviations and technical expressions which sound like gibberish to outsiders, but to IT people they are a quick and easy way of communicating complex messages – and also a way of expressing membership of the group. Codes in national cultures are discussed in Chapter 5.

Members within a culture generally follow the shared codes, but there is also always a measure of freedom to act, in which the individual person can break some of the unwritten rules without being excluded. Every member will express his cultural membership in his own way.

The cultural encounter

Culture is like a tailwind on a bicycle path. We only notice the wind when we change direction and find it going against us. We are unaware of our culture until we meet something which is different, for we have taken it for granted until then.

A cultural encounter is a communication situation where differences between the participants are felt at least by one party to be culturally determined. It may be a meeting, a job interview, a spontaneous dialogue, a teaching situation, a video conference or a telephone conversation. What is interesting about cultural encounters is not the cultural differences as such but the importance which the parties attach to culture and the cultural differences in the situation.

A cultural encounter may be planned, as when a multi-disciplinary project group is established for the purpose of solving a problem, or when a new Danish manager wants to introduce more informal knowledge sharing in a Hungarian branch. The cultural encounter may be predictable, as when a new group of colleagues of different national backgrounds are to work together. It can also arise spontaneously in a situation where a topic suddenly triggers differences among the participants.

The expression 'cultural encounter' covers situations where differences play a positive role as well as situations where they play a negative role. The latter situation is what some call a culture clash, but we find this term to be both misleading and problematic: misleading because it is not cultures which clash, but people; and problematic because it releases the parties from responsibility for the success of the encounter. We prefer to use the terms 'constructive' and 'unfruitful' cultural encounters, and remind our readers that it is possible to change the drift of the encounter as the situation proceeds.

You are the only passenger in a bus and another passenger enters. The new passenger aims deliberately for the seat next to you. If the new passenger is a friend of yours, you would expect him to choose this seat. If the situation happens in another country, and you don't know this other passenger, your first thought will be that that's obviously what people do here. But if it happens in Denmark and the passenger is a stranger, you'll wonder at his action. You may get an uncomfortable feeling of threat and want to move away a little, for the new passenger has broken a Danish cultural code which dictates physical distance.

In cultural encounters, we get a different response from the one expected and become uncertain as to the other person's intentions and how we ourselves are seen. We are confused, and a question mark is placed against our autopilot. An entire scale of different reactions can come into play when we encounter cultural differences, and they will be different in expression and strength depending on what the differences are about, how extensive the ambiguities are, and what importance the situation has. The scale below shows what can happen in human encounters, and how it looks when cultural misunderstandings are allowed to escalate to the point of conflict:

1. *Comfortable*

   A comfortable state where you experience mutual understanding, and communication proceeds smoothly above any differences.

2. *Uncertain*

   The experience of mild surprise. The communication feels a bit awkward. You feel uncertain as to what is happening. Perhaps you laugh together at your misunderstandings.

3. *Disoriented*

   You feel disoriented and uncertain that you are being understood. You are afraid of making a fool of yourself.

4. *Perplexed*

   You feel perplexed at not being able to make yourself understood, and possibly also painfully embarrassed.

5. *Shaken*

   You feel shaken and uncomfortable at realising that the other person has thoroughly misunderstood, and that you yourself or somebody else feels offended. The contact between you and the other person is about to break down.

6. *Paralysed*

   You are feeling helpless and paralysed, and feel the situation is in a deadlock and threatening – literally or metaphorically speaking. The interpersonal contact is broken.

The atmosphere may move up and down the scale during any specific encounter. The situation will balance at different points of the scale, depending on how the two parties react to emerging misunderstandings, attempts at bridge building and renewed contact. The parties may experience the situation differently, and some people will react more strongly than others to confusion and embarrassment. Some incidents trigger taboos or emotions in one or both parties, creating major tensions, and the atmosphere may jump a couple of steps on the scale. But if both parties can discuss their difficulties with a sense of humour, share them and move on, the encounter can increase emotional security rather than decrease it.

There are often several cultural differences at play at the same time in a cultural encounter. In a meeting of a multi-disciplinary project group, there will be predictable differences in professional culture; but there may also be differences of age, organisational membership, gender, nationality and ethnic background at play. It is rarely possible to predict in advance what cultural differences will emerge and come into play, or which will play a positive role and which will create misunderstandings.

The positive potential of cultural encounters

A meeting of different points of view and backgrounds holds a large positive potential for new thinking, and it demands that we shake off our habitual ways of thinking, that we look outside our normal frames of reference and leave old habits behind. Confusion and misunderstandings can sometimes stimulate us to discover new angles and produce new knowledge. The creative potential in a cultural meeting can emerge at different points on the scale, from the stage of comfortable and humorous questioning of what we take for granted, to somewhere up the scale, where misunderstandings have triggered a personal sense of embarrassment.

Having one's usual way of thinking shaken at an unexpected moment is not always a pleasant experience, and new thinking is automatically the result of it. The Danish innovation expert Susanne Justesen developed the concept of 'innoversity' in 2001. It covers innovation generated from diversity of age, gender, national background, education and ethnicity. Justesen discovered five driving forces which can turn an encounter of differences into new thinking, creativity and innovation:

Capacity to absorb – that is the ability to grasp and respond. The potential for learning and developing new knowledge is greater in groups with participants of different backgrounds than in groups with participants of similar backgrounds.

Necessary variety – the more backgrounds and perspectives are represented among the participants, the more combinations of knowledge and methods there will be.

Access to larger networks – participants of different ages and educational, national, ethnic and organisational backgrounds provide access to many different sources of external knowledge.

Creative destruction – customary routines must be broken down to make room for something new to grow. Different perspectives are important because they spur reflection and question the usual routines.

Broader perspective on problem solving – as different approaches can break down the usual routines and improve problem solving methods and processes.

When an inter-organisational or a cross-disciplinary group is established to create better problem solving methods, the result is a deliberately planned cultural encounter with the aim of achieving positive results. A company intending to develop a new product for its customers may, for example, establish a group which includes people who know and understand customers' needs, people with commercial expertise in the field, and people with an insight into the necessary technology and production.

Cultural encounters can also result in new ideas by accident as spontaneous by-products of a situation. It may be new members who upset the usual way of doing things by unwittingly asking uncomfortable questions, or it may be disagreements within the group which spark off a discussion and the questioning of usual practices. The question of whether uncomfortable questions and disagreements will lead to positive results depends on the power relationships in the situation. Differences within a group do not automatically lead to new thinking. Whether they do depends heavily on how group members experience and handle their cultural differences. Chapter 4 will explore how good merging processes depend on a conscious and planned approach to cultural encounters.

Two understandings of culture in a cultural encounter

There will often be two different understandings of culture at play in a cultural encounter – at least at the beginning. The parties will typically use the complex understanding of culture to understand and describe themselves, while they will apply the descriptive understanding to explain what they find 'strange'.

When describing ourselves, we tend to use the knowledge that we are multifaceted individuals, the product of and members of several cultures, and that in some situations one part of our identities is important, while in other situations other parts will be activated.

On the other hand, we use the simpler descriptive understanding of culture without thinking when describing someone who is different from ourselves. We look at the others from the outside and describe them from one perspective, namely their points of obvious difference from ourselves. For example:"Our German colleagues like to be in control and make rules for everything." "Those in R&D are always so creative, but it's all airy fairy – they have no sense of reality or common sense, not like us in production." "Those from company X are so used to hierarchy and formality."

The descriptive understanding of culture can also be used to describe one's own culture, for example "We nurses believe…" "We Norwegians are…" Sentences such as these describe a notional community distinct from all others and ignore internal differences within the group.

It is of course somewhat misleading to say that the two different understandings of culture are present in cultural encounters, for gradually, as the two parties build up familiarity and mutual understanding, they will discover more sides to each other and take a more nuanced look at each other. But this does not happen automatically, as strong dynamics are at play below the surface.

Preconceptions and stereotypes

In a meeting of people of different cultural backgrounds, it is the different practices which the parties will notice first, but in a problematic meeting like the one in the following example, the different perceptions of self and preconceptions of others become important, and will lead the parties to interpret the same practice differently.

The Swedish industrial firm had a deputy manager who was highly respected and popular, and had a large and vital area of responsibility – we'll call him Alfred. He had been in the company for many years. He had started there straight from school, had completed his apprenticeship as a metalworker in the engineering workshop, had first advanced to works manager, and gradually worked his way up through the hierarchy while educating himself further. As deputy manager he was appointed chairman of a working group which was to prepare a key area for the merger with a French company. There were other people in the group at his level from both companies. The group members started their first meeting by introducing themselves and learning something about each others' experiences in the field so as to apply the various expertise present in the fast-working group in the best possible manner. But Alfred met a response which was entirely different from the one he was used to. The French managers all presented themselves with abbreviated titles and university degrees in engineering science, which meant absolutely nothing to this Swede, and they were clearly embarrassed and confused when finding that Alfred had started as a metalworker and had no university degree. Alfred found that his opinions didn't count as much as those of the others. When mentioning practical examples, he was sometimes met by silence from the French side of the table. The French group complained at home. They felt that by appointing a non-academic chairman, the Swedish company had failed to treat the area and the group with the proper respect and priority. Alfred felt he had been badly misunderstood at the first meeting. His competence had been questioned, and he felt shaken and uncertain as to whether he would be able to discharge his task as chairman of the group in a satisfactory manner in the given situation.

There were obvious differences in the practices of the two companies with respect to what was required to make a managerial career. These practices had their roots in the differences between the French and Swedish national cultures, but they were probably reinforced by the two companies' own histories and cultures. Added to this were differences between the engineering community's sense of pride and status as compared with that of the metalworkers, and the two professional groups' preconceptions of each other. However, both parties felt that the other party treated them with disrespect, and the cause of this was their highly divergent interpretations of their own and the other party's practice in terms of legitimate qualifications for a managerial position and how to show respect for others.

This cultural encounter would have been less frustrating and less disruptive for the group's work if they had been better informed of each other's cultural traits. It is wise to prepare for an encounter with other cultures by learning something about each other's differences. To do so gives a basis for attempting to understand statements, reactions and proposals from the point of view of the other side, rather than being limited to interpretations based on one's own culture alone. Such background knowledge can also be used to improve our own communication in the 'foreign' culture in order to reduce the risk of being misunderstood or breaking important rules in the other culture, and so being felt to be disrespectful. But it is important to remember that descriptions of the other party are not absolute truths. Labelling each other does not improve communication.

Putting everything different into simplified categories is one of the ways in which we manage to make sense of our everyday experiences, and stereotypes are an unavoidable consequence of this. It is necessary to simplify and structure our surroundings, and we are wired to sort millions of impressions into meaningful categories. Otherwise we would go mad trying to make sense of all the impressions we are constantly receiving. Building up general categories is a way of handling our surroundings, but when the categories become rigid and value-laden, they become stereotypes. Many studies show that we humans are very quick to over-generalise people from groups which are different from ourselves, and some preconceptions are stereotypes and prejudices.

A married couple, Matilda and Samuel, were born in Ghana, had lived 12 years in Denmark, and were running a cleaning business. One Friday late afternoon they came to a house where they locked themselves in as usual, turned off the security alarm and started cleaning the house. Just before they had finished that Friday, they saw three police cars in the street outside, and officers with dogs were swarming up the garden path. They went out to meet the men and were met by a loud shout: "What are you doing here?" The next minutes were chaotic. The two shocked cleaners tried to explain why they were in the house and to ask why the police were there. But the officers shouted that they should keep quiet or they would be fined for disturbing the peace. The police refused to believe the couple's explanations even though they were able to show their keys to the house. Fortunately, the owner of the house arrived home. The misunderstanding was cleared up and the police left the place. It turned out that the neighbour had reported thieves in the house, as the stereotypical understanding of two dark-skinned people in a house in an up-market neighbourhood is 'thieves', or possibly 'thieves posing as cleaners'. (The newspaper *Politiken*, 21 September 2006)

Communication is normally the route to get beyond stereotypes in cultural encounters, but in this case the misunderstandings were not cleared away despite the two cleaners' explanations to the police officers, as the latter's interpretation of the situation was so deadlocked that only the intervention of a third person (the owner of the house) was able to effect a change.

The communicative process

It is necessary to explore the communicative process itself in order to understand what takes place between two people in a cultural encounter. When two people communicate with each other, a circular process comes into play in which the parties are constantly influencing each other and reacting to each other – consciously and unconsciously.

While one party is speaking, she is also noticing how the other party appears to receive what she is saying, and she adjusts her words to the reaction she feels she is getting from the other party. The man listens and looks at the talking woman, but he is also – consciously or unconsciously – communicating a response to the woman via his body language, eyes, facial expressions and gestures. And when she stops talking and he starts, the same mechanisms continue but the other way around. Communicating with another person is thus a process of mutual influence. Communicating is not merely the dispatch and receipt of a series of messages, as via two radio transmitters which are not affected by the communication. When two people communicate, there is an unbroken process of interpretation and adjustment relative to the signals received from the other party.

Not to communicate is not possible. We may think that silence, reticence or fading into the wallpaper has a neutral effect, but sometimes the words which are not spoken or the response which is not given has as strong an effect as a vigorous reaction.

We all communicate through individual filters which are formed by our experiences, personality, background, values, education, goals, insight into ourselves and interests. The filters also include our self-awareness and preconceptions of the other party, our views and expectations of, and our experiences with, the other person, based on the knowledge and relationship we have with that other person.

The term 'filter' should be understood as something dynamic, changeable and 'from-where-I'm-standing-right-now'. Our filter is different from situation to situation depending on which pattern of interpretation is activated in precisely that context. When a manager meets an employee from the same company, the filter will function in one way, but if the manager is meeting his son's teacher, the filter has changed. The filter is also updated in light of the continuing pattern of responses received from each other.

We are only rarely aware of our filters when communicating, and our interpretation of the situation and the other party takes place largely at subconscious level. We basically communicate with other people as if they were like ourselves. We say something which seems meaningful to ourselves. Similarly, we can only receive messages from other people via our personal filter. We decode both words and body language via our filter in order to make meaning out of it all.

It is the case in all communicative acts that we only understand the other person when we understand what he wanted to say. There are different methods for improving our communication, and they are all about being interested in our own and the other person's filter, and being able to discuss this openly with one another. Putting things in other words is one way of checking understanding: "I understand this to mean that…" or asking "Please explain to me what you heard me say. I may not have expressed myself very clearly."

Communication in intercultural encounters

Communication across cultural divides is particularly challenging because the differences between people's filters are greater. The decoding of each other's messages presents a problem, so misunderstandings can arise. When, for example, the finance and accounts staff are communicating with other professional groups, their technical terms and abbreviations are not readily understood, so they have to unwrap (= decode) their message and explain it in other words to enable others to understand it. Whether the complications of communicating will lead to new thinking or to more problems will depend on the situation.

As long as the communicative act proceeds within a single culture, the parties can attach the same meaning to events and statements, and the communication can proceed with little problem. But in order to communicate in a cultural encounter, the parties have to negotiate meaning across different ways of seeing things, as the parties have different frames of reference, and an effort is required before they can be certain that they will understand what the other person is trying to say. And what do those words "we understand each other" really mean? We can understand one another, but we have to negotiate meaning at several levels and dig down well below our immediate perceptions.

When encountering a new professional jargon or a foreign language, the parties know that they will have to make an effort in order to be able to understand each other. But in situations where different

(Dahl, 2001)

expectations and preconceptions of the other party come into play, we may well start out by believing that we understand each other, and that is when misunderstandings can take us entirely by surprise, with serious consequences. Chapter 3 explores clear and overlooked cultural differences between professional groups in more depth.

Cultural self-perception is a person's experience of his cultural community in the situation. Self-perception and preconceptions are interdependent. When one party begins to describe the other party as an American HR person from IBM, she is also beginning a narrative of herself. Self-perception is created in the situation by comparison with another culture: there is something which I am definitely not, and some traits which we share. Self-perception is generally seen through idyllic glasses and based on ideals of how things ought to be. What is special about cultural self-perception is that it appears exclusively in the encounter with someone else. Only in the construction of the 'other' are we able to create such an idealised image of ourselves.

Stereotypes are self-reinforcing

The images of ourselves and the other party which we bring with us to a cultural encounter are not merely innocent deceptions. If the parties entertain stereotypical views of each other, they can influence the other party to act the part. Stereotypes deadlock the horizon of our expectations and easily become self-affirming. This is because they enter into the filter through which we send and understand. The views and expectations we have of the other party influence our actions and our interpretations of the other party's actions, and this is how a self-reinforcing circle can begin. As a young man in a Danish activation project for the unemployed said: "It's difficult to show what I'm good at, for at the start they saw me only as a young man of Arabic background and in need of help."

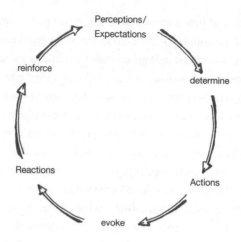

Stereotypes can be both negative and positive, and it follows that the self-reinforcing circle can also become positive or negative. Stereotypes can be difficult to get rid of. This is because we find it easy to remember an expression or a scene which confirms our stereotypes. We have firm expectations as to what will happen, and as the circle shows, we contribute to provoking the reactions in the other party which our stereotypes have pre-programmed us to expect. When, on the other hand, something happens to contradict our stereotypes, we are often too blinded to realise what is happening. We ignore the incident, forget it, or explain it away as the exception that proves the rule. Bookkeepers are supposed to be very well-organised, so if we meet a messy and untidy bookkeeper, he has merely had a bad day.

Feelings and other uncontrollable aspects of cultural encounters

Cultural encounters involve non-stop negotiation of the meaning of the parties' communication. This is not, however, a controlled process, but a search process where the next step can't be predicted, and where rational considerations and irrational reactions intertwine.

Very few people like being defined from the outside and being seen only as representatives of a group, but it is particularly unpleasant when we are exposed to negative stereotyping because others think they have the right to define us. We feel that parts of our identity are being enlarged and criticised, while other parts are called into doubt or overlooked. It is particularly crucial if power play is involved, so that the offending behaviour is consciously or unconsciously a demonstration of power, or will at least be felt in that way by the victim. It is not always possible or appropriate to object in the situation if, for example, the offending person is the boss or the interviewer in a job interview. The person with less power will feel disagreements more strongly than the other party.

One thing is that people react emotionally to being defined by outsiders, but we also react emotionally if we look at a situation completely within our own cultural perceptions. Unless we are conscious of our own cultural traits, we will take them for granted and consider them the only right way of doing things. We may even think them ordinary common sense. "Culture is dictatorial unless understood and examined," as the British culture expert E.T. Hall puts it. Unless we are able to take a step back and talk about our culture, we will react when an unwritten rule is broken: "This is all wrong!"

Those parts of our cultural traits which were imprinted in childhood and stored in body and brain independently of language are particularly strong. When a rule is broken in this field, we react emotionally and possibly also with physical displeasure. Many Scandinavian people refuse to eat local food when travelling if the menu includes grasshoppers or snakes, and some Muslims are nauseated by the smell of pork.

It is easier to change attitudes and convictions than deep-seated feelings of right and wrong. Strongly charged prejudices against other people are generally the result of emotional imprinting early in life. Some white Americans who grew up in the southern states thus say that although, intellectually speaking, they have long since abandoned racial prejudices about black Americans – prejudices which they imbibed with their mother's milk – they still feel physical discomfort when shaking hands with a black person. Such strong emotional reactions are most dominant when we are in autopilot mode because the body then reacts automatically via embedded routine reactions. These reactions will not, however, disappear the first time we switch to manual control and prepare mentally for the unaccustomed handshake. More handshakes, new experiences and a greater personal acquaintance with black people are required before the automatic reaction disappears.

One aspect of the communicative process becomes extra strong when we communicate across cultural divides, namely that we judge other people's communication on the effect it has, while we assess our own communication on its underlying motive. An example of this is when we hear somebody being criticised for something they've said and they answer "But all I meant was…" We feel unfairly treated when we are misunderstood and our good intentions go unrecognised – and this applies both ways. Cultural encounters generate many irrational responses, and we are not aware of them all.

As noted earlier, the interesting point about cultural encounters is not the cultural differences as such, but the importance which the parties attach to culture in the situation, sometimes overstating the importance of cultural differences and at other times ignoring them.

Culture as an explanation

It happens in intercultural communications that the parties use culture as the explanation of why they disagree. Culture is sometimes used as an easy excuse for abandoning responsibility for pursuing a solution. "If we have problems because our cultures are different, we can't do anything about it." "We can't help that we're different". This response is similar to referring to 'bad chemistry' when two people can't work together. It is abandoning every attempt to establish genuine contact and find a way of working together. Referring to culture can also remove attention from the real problem, which may be a battle over interests or territory. Attaching a cultural label and a cultural membership to another person can be a demonstration of power.

A Danish survey of school classes of mixed ethnic backgrounds showed that the young people of Danish ethnic background as well as those of other ethnic backgrounds created barriers against mixed ethnic groupings. The youngsters stressed a small number of differences about each other (religion, clothes and drinking habits) and imagined a string of other differences which in reality did not exist. Although they mixed every day, they saw each other in light of their differences – imagined differences (Klinker & Rasmussen). This is an example of the point that more communication does not automatically lead to better cultural understanding, but can also lead to the use of culture as an explanation and excuse.

Peter became manager of a workplace where the majority of workers were women. After a while, problems began to appear, and at a seminar on cooperation, Peter was told that the cause of the problems was the big change it had been for the workers to get a male boss. They believed they could feel that he was used to male-dominated workplaces, and that he did not fit in with them. Peter's reaction was frustration. "This is not about my being a male at all, but that I demand more efficiency. A female manager would also have made those demands in the situation in which we are. It is annoying that the workers believe this to be about males and females. I want to be seen as the manager, but not as a male manager as I can't change my gender."

There was a strong pre-perception of Peter as a male boss, and some of his actions and personality traits were interpreted by the workers on the basis of their perception of male culture. The surrounding preconceptions of gender differences meant that they saw him differently from the way he wished to be seen, and how could he possibly escape the role he had thus been allotted?

In Chapter 4 we explore in more detail how culture is often misused as an explanation and excuse for problems arising in connection with mergers.

Culture ignored – cultural blindness

Misunderstandings can arise because we believe that we have more things in common with people from other cultures than we actually have. The American culture expert Nancy Adler calls this phenomenon 'projective similarity', and says it is a trap in intercultural communication because it can make us act inappropriately or inefficiently. It is a form of cultural blindness which means that we either do not discover at all, or we do not want to see that different perspectives, codes and ways of acting are present. "Of course I understand you, but you don't understand me" is an example of cultural blindness. We explore cultural blindness in more detail in relation to different professional groups in Chapter 3.

"He didn't come across to me as particularly honest, or can there have been something wrong with his self-confidence? Didn't you notice that it was very difficult to make eye contact with him?" The two Britons were exchanging experiences from their first meeting with their new Japanese colleague, and they were clearly not aware that direct eye contact is used more sparingly in several Asian cultures than among northern Europeans and Americans. Scandinavians often interpret frequent and intensive eye contact as a sign of open and honest communication. We receive some body signals without thinking, but we notice it as soon as something isn't quite as it should be. We find it difficult, for example, to erase our discomfort from a limp handshake or from not being able to establish the eye contact which makes us feel secure.

It is important to be aware that cultural differences may be involved before we interpret the situation unilaterally and draw conclusions on the basis of our own cultural yardstick – or apply our own physical yardstick without thought, as the following real life example shows.

In September 1999, NASA lost its Mars Climate Orbiter, which was valued at $125 million. The satellite had been developed in a partnership between NASA (US) and Lockheed Martin (UK), and was to have entered an orbit around Mars after an outward journey of 289 days. Unfortunately the satellite came too close to the planet and crashed into the surface. The reason turned out to be a calculation error due to the use of different measuring units. NASA's laboratories used the metric system, kilos and metres, while Lockheed Martin used the British units, pounds and inches. Engineers from the two organisations had exchanged calculations and figures over a long partnership and had done so in the expectation that the other group was using the same units as they themselves did. Nobody was criticised for having committed the error and the incident was hushed up. (CNN, 'Metric mishap caused loss of NASA orbiter', 30 September 1999, http://www.cnn.com/TECH/space/9909/30/mars.metric.02)

This is an incredible and extremely expensive example of cultural blindness, and of how bad things can turn out when we take something in our own culture for granted. None of the engineers were able to imagine that the other company's engineers used other measuring units, so nobody checked this banal but crucial condition of their partnership and their complicated calculations. They were all intent on their common task and all their mutual similarities, and evidently blind to the mutual differences. We trust that in later partnership projects in space exploration, culture experts will have been brought in to complement engineering experts.

A professional comment on the case of the Danish cartoons crisis

There are situations in which cultural differences present a particular challenge. This is when we hit or get too close to a taboo, something particularly sacrosanct, inviolable or forbidden. This was the situation when an inviolable thing in one culture clashed head on with an inviolable thing from another culture in the case of the cartoons crisis, namely the freedom of expression in Denmark and the Muslim ban on depicting the prophet Muhammed. The problem began in October 2005, when the Danish newspaper *Jyllands-Posten* published 12 cartoons on Islam and the prophet Muhammed, leading to misunderstandings, diplomatic tugs-of-war, and ultimately to the burning of Danish embassies in the Middle East. Tragically, more than 50 lives were lost in demonstrations abroad, and there was a substantial loss of income for Danish exporters. The case ran a rather complicated course through international politics with many examples of cultural misunderstandings between the parties, many irrational reactions, and both national and international politicisations exploiting these. Countless people became involved as events unfolded, and they probably had many different ways of intervening, but some main features did stand out.

The case is an example of how important cultural understanding is, and how quickly things can escalate if misunderstandings and conflicts are not stopped. The case would not have escalated to the extent it did if the disagreements had been discussed face to face between the most important parties as soon as they had appeared. The first few months witnessed a string of different actions which served to make the cultural encounter increasingly unconstructive, and to escalate the conflict. An obvious example was the Danish prime minister's refusal to attend a meeting to which a group of Middle Eastern ambassadors had invited him, a refusal which he explained by stating that he knew what they would say, and he disagreed with their views. Both parties ascribed motives to each other, expressed stereotyped perceptions of each other's cultures, and gave simplified explanations to complex problems, thus presenting themselves in the best possible light. Nobody listened to the other party's views, and there was little understanding of the other party's situation and perspectives. The other side was blamed for the escalation of the situation, and a battle was fought for the right to define what is important and what is not – was it about freedom of expression or about the taboo against images of the prophet? It was a battle of power, serving only to deepen the differences, misunderstandings or prejudices with each party insisting that its own viewpoint was the only right one. It was an example of a lack of cultural understanding and a lack of interest in cultural bridge-building, and quite apart from all this, the case was used by all parties to highlight vastly different agendas.

The sequence of events in this case clearly demonstrates the point that cultural understanding is not simply about tolerance and tolerating each other's differences. It is necessary to enter into dialogue about each other's actions and underlying values. We have to be interested in the background on which 'the others' act and think. Otherwise we are showing a lack of respect. We must tell each other in open dialogue what we think about each other's actions and how we interpret each other's actions in relation to our own set values. Only then can we turn the cultural encounter to constructive use and gain greater cultural understanding of each other.

The case of the cartoons is an example of the consequences of unconstructive cultural encounters at the level of society and on the stage of international politics; but this book focuses on cultural encounters in the world of business and the workplace, and the three chapters which now follow will explore a different cultural field and propose ideas on how to work in a culturally intelligent manner in business and in the workplace. These theme chapters will treat one cultural difference at a time as if they appear in isolation in pure form – which they never do. There will always be several different cultural differences among the participants and they often intermingle, while at other times the focus may be directed on one cultural dimension, for example professional differences.

3/

WHEN PROFESSIONAL CULTURES MEET IN THE WORKPLACE

A company's survival and development depends on cross-professional problem solving, knowledge sharing and innovation, and this is only possible if the different professions meet each other in a constructive manner

In the Scandinavian countries, focus has been increasingly directed on the necessity of developing strategies and competences aimed at making the small Scandinavian economies competitive.

> We will only be able to maintain our high Danish living standard in a global economy by staying ahead of our competitors – in thought and action. To stay ahead, we must be more creative and innovative than the rest of the world. This is why economic security in the society of the future is not just about knowledge and education, but also about an entirely new work culture where new thinking and its heroes are valued.
>
> Lindholm & Møller, 2004

This point was made by the Danish management researchers Mikael R. Lindholm and Kim Møller among others, and it is no less relevant now.

A company's survival and development depends on cross-professional problem solving, knowledge sharing and innovation, and this is only possible if the different professions meet each other in a constructive manner. Every profession has its own approach, its own special understanding and its own competences, and many tasks are so complex that to solve them, a multi-professional forum must be established. The argument can be made that in the fully developed knowledge society, all professions are each others' support professions.

The different professions must enter into creative and productive interaction – not merely to prevent controversies and ensure a smooth production process, but just as much to harness the full driving force of the different professions and to realise the potential latent in their encounters. Cultural intelligence is required for this.

It is therefore somewhat surprising that so little focus is directed at professional cultures and ways in which to ensure that they meet constructively. Professional cultures are generally only mentioned in terms of stereotypes, 'the legal eagle', 'a bookkeeper mentality', 'a schoolmasterly bearing', 'a bedside manner'.

It is not the profession or the professional competences we refer to when using such terms, but rather some cultural traits from the relevant professional practice and its practitioners which make us feel annoyed or enthusiastic. "We were just talking about trying to appoint some humanities graduates next time!"

In this chapter, we pinpoint some of the factors which lift professional partnerships up to a level above the individual professions, thus promoting better problem solving, knowledge sharing and innovation. We discuss the nature of professional practice, the function of professional cultures, and what happens when professional cultures encounter each other. We present a model illustrating different types of professional cooperation and we look at different arenas where cross-professional work is carried out. Towards the end of the chapter we present some methods for developing cross-professional collaboration in a culturally intelligent way.

Professionalisms

In order to discuss what happens when different professionalisms and professional cultures meet, it is necessary to look first at what professionalism is. Professionalism manifests itself in trades, professions and functions.

A trade or profession is a delimited pool of knowledge, competences and methods, the aim of which is to perform a particular type of task. A profession can be identical with educational or vocational qualifications, for example engineer, carpenter or police officer, while at other times it may designate a job, for example salesman, bookkeeper or teacher.

A *profession* is a particular role with inherent authority and powers, but also with an inherent responsibility. The term 'profession' was originally associated with the traditional social institutions: the courts, the church, the military, and educational institutions, but it is now used more broadly. An extensive process of professionalisation is currently in progress in Scandinavia and other European countries as many professions and professional groups, for example several medium-length courses of training such as nursing, social work and teaching are renamed and recoined 'professional bachelor degrees' and the courses are given a more academic direction.

A *function* is a particular role in a company, to which is attached a set of duties and partial responsibility for the performance of the main task; and organisations organise themselves internally so as to maximise the various professional contributions and the manner in which professional practices are used. This may involve a division into business areas, production lines or matrices. A bachelor of commerce may be working in the finance department in direct extension of his education, or in Human Resources because this department has a need for specific competences, or because this particular bachelor has some special experience. On the basis of her education and profession, the senior registrar has the 'right' to decide which treatment the patient should be given, but when she changes her role from senior registrar at the hospital to production manager in a drug company, the emphasis shifts from profession to function. She now uses her professional qualifications in a different manner, and will be met by entirely different expectations regarding her professional practice.

There can be differences in how the private and public sectors judge professionalism. Companies have their own systems for assessing and approving an applicant's professionalism, and approval is geared to the professional content and scope of the job. The entry ticket to the public sector has traditionally been an examination and possibly relevant experience, while in the private sector, it is traditionally results and performance that open the doors.

The manager of a medium-size production company puts it clearly: "When I need a new man, the first thing I look for is his credibility. Does he look what he says he can do and will be in a manner so that I'm convinced? Has he achieved anything? It may be in an entirely different field; that doesn't matter so much. And if I appoint him, I want to see results – quite quickly! Let me put it straight: *What can you do? What will you do? And where are the results which prove that you can and will?*"

This cultural borderline between the private and the public sectors is clearly softening along the edges. This isn't happening without cuts or blows, but in the case below we meet a middle manager who benefited from the fact that formal university-trained thinking habits have spread deep inside industries and sectors where they were never seen before.

"Five or six years ago, I was merely an electrician. If you had then suggested to me that I should take a university degree I would have thought you were having me on! And now I've finished my MBA, and there are at least five others in the firm who are also doing all sorts of different courses at university or business college. This is because the company is focusing on continuing education, and I really feel that they mean it. I've had great support all the way through. I'm still an electrician. I haven't turned into something else. But I'm an electrician with an MBA. I'm still making measuring equipment, but now I do so with professional pride and confidence!"

Professionalism and profession also have an individual dimension, a human necessity. The individual human person largely finds his awareness of self and his human worth in his profession and in his professional roles and relations. Adulthood, full and valid membership and autonomy are awarded by professional colleagues in the group. That is to say, we are accepted into the community and we practice our membership of it.

For the rest of this chapter, we do not distinguish between trade, profession and function. They will be discussed under one as professions and professionalisms.

The function of professional cultures – how and why is culture a part of professionalism?

A professional culture is a characteristic manner of practising one's profession. It is a set of ways of relating to colleagues of the same and other professions, and it is based on special competences, a particular socialisation and disciplining process. Every profession has its own rationale and its own function, its own methods and competences – what we can call the nature of the profession – and these are the firm substances of a professional culture. Cultures are forms of practice, and a professional culture is the way in which professionalism is translated into practice. A professional culture is a form of professional 'good manners'. It is the manner in which the profession adjusts to the surrounding world. A professional culture draws a line between what belongs to the profession and what falls outside, and therefore has no validity in a professional sense. A professional culture differentiates. It includes something and somebody, and it excludes something and somebody. In this regard there is no difference between professional cultures and culture in other contexts.

Professional cultures have two functions. The first is to make it possible to practice the profession, and it places the practitioners of the profession in a position where they have clout. The second function is to create identity for the practitioner and membership of the professional community.

Let us consider the first function. We find the most obvious professional cultures in the old professions which constituted the social institutions – the church, military, courts, police, and health services. If a clergyman is to represent the greatest of all authorities, God, it is only reasonable that his role and function is endowed with cultural attributes which stress that he is now a full and valid representative of the highest authority. It is important that the rest of us should feel safe in leaving the authority and the decisions to him.

The same sense of security must be present before we are willing to place our lives in the doctor's hands. We are unwilling to place the power of life and death in the hands of an ordinary person unless that person is imbued with very special qualities, so we associate that ordinary person with an authority and wisdom which exceeds human capacity.

Professions where competition has been a fundamental condition from the very beginning have also developed obvious cultural practices. The craft guilds have had an ingenious system of cultural codes, actions and attributes which served to protect and develop the professions and their legitimate practitioners ever since the early Middle Ages. The guilds are one of the early examples of deliberate branding, refinement and corporate politics at professional level. The words for 'guild' in the European languages all contain the meaning 'community' or 'mutually binding community'. And as we know, trade unions now attempt to make use of this inheritance in entirely new contexts.

Professional cultural features have their origins in something practical. A group manager who had worked for many years in the production of steel components told of his experiences with the practical sources of culture. He had always looked at the sales and marketing department as a boring place for dull dogs and fusspots. He had also seen the sales staff as having a somewhat laid-back and don't-care attitude. It was only when the group manager took part in a management course with managerial staff from the sales department that he realised that the physical environment in production made it necessary to communicate in a special way. So many people were moving about in production, and the noise level was – or rather used to be – very loud. The air was often full of water vapour and the workers wore hearing protection and safety glasses. In response to this environment, people in production had learnt to speak in very loud voices or to shout, and to use numerous gestures and physical touches such as a slap on the shoulder. Manners were quieter and far less demonstrative in the sales and marketing department because that was more appropriate to the work done there.

Given their function, it is also practical that the professionals working in the company's accounts department should be accurate, follow the fixed procedures and check their decimal points. The accounts employee who moved from the budgets and accounts team to finance strategy and development had to get used to speaking in very round figures – a practice which she found irresponsible and unprofessional at first.

The second important function of professional cultures is to create an identity for the practitioner and a sense of membership of the professional community. Most people will remember, from their own fledgling professional days, the effort they took to imitate the professional community to which they wanted an entry ticket. The effort was not only concentrated on acquiring the professional competences, but just as much on training the professional cultural practice. A retired branch manager remembers how he wore his only suit to shiny threads during his first year as a trainee because he almost lived in it. It was important for him to send the signal 'banker' both to himself and his surroundings – even on his way to the baker on Sunday mornings for fresh bread rolls. The same thing happens to the nursing student who changes the term 'womb' to 'uterus' on her first day in nursing school, and to the office trainee in the shipping line who says "We in the shipping line" from day one. These changes are constructive and a necessary step in development, just as it is when a four-year-old imitates the practices of the adults.

Professional membership gives the practitioner the crucial mandate which enables him to assume his chosen professionalism and enter into the attractive community in a binding and convincing manner. A series of cultural exchanges and negotiations are involved when the role is granted by an organisation or profession and accepted by the person who is to fill the role and the function. We expect what we call 'adult behaviour' in a professional role, and the idea of what that behaviour is, is formed in the profession's mould. The old rule set for the behaviour of higher officials – also during off-hours – is a good example.

The professional role and the organisation we belong to become the horizon within which we see ourselves and reality, and find meaning. The western European background culture grants membership via education and job. We are not really 'adults' before we are on the payroll of an organisation.

Different types of people are attracted by different types of profession. Professions requiring accuracy and care will attract some, while others will feel attracted to jobs requiring a willingness to take risks and an ability not to lose oneself in details. When we 'are' our profession, we are so thoroughly integrated into it that it can be difficult to distinguish between the competences and rationales of the profession – what we call the nature of the profession – and what is its culture for better or worse. The 'good' cultural features are those which facilitate the profession, enabling its most outstanding performances. The 'bad' cultural features are those which function as a defence or evasion on the part of its practitioners. It is generally these features which distort the profession so that it appears as a professional caricature, frozen in an exaggerated form.

People with a professional background are thus not merely competent, but also 'cultured' in a professional sense. This 'culturalisation' facilitates relations within one's own profession, but it can make it harder to handle relations across professional fields:

A former officer of the defence forces took part in a cross-professional and cross-sectional project for a while. He was head-hunted to the project because of his language qualifications and experience from having worked in the Middle East. At some stage the project ran into difficulties, and so did the officer because he 'placed responsibility' for the problems with the members of the project group who had spoken in favour of omitting a traditional risk analysis. The officer's action aroused anger in the project group, especially when the officer added that it was a general problem that his analytical competences were not adequately recognised.

It is likely that the officer brought a military professional culture with him, and that the rules of this culture demanded that 'responsibility be placed' with suitable punishment, or at least consequences, for the person responsible. It is also likely that detailed analysis, followed by guidelines and control in accordance with the results of the analysis, was another important part of the officer's culture, a professional cultural how-to-do. These preferences on the part of the officer were in sharp contrast to the more democratic negotiating culture of the majority of the group members. The officer simply had entirely different criteria for relevance than did his colleagues. It is more than likely that this difference in the officer's professional culture could have given rise to a creative challenging of each other, and could have improved the process considerably if the project group's cultural intelligence had been better developed. In the event, the officer left the group shortly after this controversy.

Our basic principle is that any process whatsoever in a workplace which contributes to the total solution – communicative, operative, financial – has a cultural band wound tightly around the professional functional practice. And this is where we are touching on the necessity of cultural intelligence in the meeting of professions.

When professional cultures meet

We are leaving the industrial society and its work-based handling of materials at full speed, heading for the knowledge society based on our ability to handle material, psychological, organisational and social complexity. The answer to the growing external complexity is to develop a matching internal complexity in the individual employee, in the group and in the organisation.

Qvortrup, 2004

This is a conclusion from the former director of the Danish Knowledge Lab, Lars Qvortrup. One of the crucial challenges in the management of knowledge production is to get different fields of knowledge to meet in a fruitful manner. It is on the boundaries of, and in the transitions between, professional areas and professional practitioners that the unexpected happens and ideas emerge. We know that learning and innovation occur when we hit a boundary or cross a line between the well-known on the one hand and the unknown on the other, at the point where truisms fall away and routines are inadequate and the logic breaks up, the point where we are no longer in the centre of our understanding and local common sense.

Values are attached to the boundaries between professionalisms, and this is why an enormous energy and engagement is ready for release along these boundaries. When practitioners encounter each other across a professional boundary line, the outcome may be one of two. If the encounter fails, the boundary line acts like a no-man's land, a barrier or a trench. The energy is transformed into border clashes or retreat.

If the encounter succeeds, the boundary line acts like an interface, and the energy in the field stimulates positive engagement. Such a constructive encounter clears a path for:

- Applying and combining knowledge and methods across tasks and situations.
- Balancing our professional and functional authority – a balance which is achieved when the practitioners possess enough professional independence and self-confidence within their own fields to be able to put their professional egos aside and show respect and sensitivity to alien professional fields as well as to their authority and quality criteria.
- Moving into unknown territory and drawing the map as we go – it is necessary to be able to focus attention on problems in a new field which are difficult to penetrate, and to have the energy and the discipline to plan and carry through the attempt (Rasmussen, 2002).

Let us take a closer look at the constructive professional cultural encounters where we assume that knowledge sharing, innovation and cross-professional problem solving are created.

Knowledge sharing

When we are confronted with somebody else's entirely different understanding of a situation, a potential for knowledge sharing emerges. An example of this is Jesper's experience:

Jesper, who is technical manager in a big company, reaped a personal experience of learning at the boundary line. He took part in a project management course in a group where many different functions and professions were represented. Jesper was disappointed and impatient at the end of the first two-day module. The expectations he had had of the course had not been met at all: "After two full days we hadn't been given a single tool to take home with us!" Jesper then remembers how the evaluation which filled the last thirty minutes of the course had fundamentally changed his assessment of the module and of how he had profited from it. "It was only when I heard the others' answers to the questions 'What in particular are you taking away with you?' and 'What did you find most inspiring for you?' and 'What are you now going home to do…?' that I was able to see the two days in an entirely different light. I learnt more from that evaluation than I had done in the two previous days."

At first, the course had made no sense to Jesper. His technician's culture had made it impossible for him to find his directions and organise the activities of the two days into logical units in his own head. The other members of the group had a very different understanding. They gained a sense of some new structures during the course. They felt that a pattern was emerging. They were enthusiastically juggling the many interesting questions which had arisen – and they saw all this as knowledge. Jesper, on the other hand, brought a culture with him to the course which understood knowledge as something made explicit, tested and fixed. Jesper's cultural intelligence was evident in his willingness to let go of his local common sense and see himself and the situation in a new perspective, and use an entirely different yardstick. Knowledge has a way of turning up like an uninvited guest.

Despite the fact that surprises are daily fare, many project leaders still do not like being confronted with 'unplanned' knowledge. This chance of learning more is still seen rather as a sign of poor planning, which makes them feel ashamed and which they make a hurried effort to forget.

Amtoft & Vestergaard, 2003

The attention paid to knowledge sharing by an organisation is evident in many ways and in different degrees. The knowing and learning organisation introduces work routines into cross-professional meetings which enable the exchange of methods, information, experiences and perspectives. It has procedures which ensure that new knowledge can grow out of the knowledge which is already available, so that no resources are wasted on parallel knowledge production in hermetically sealed tanks. The organisation is not prepared to start from scratch every time. The organisation also has procedures for circulating new knowledge round the company and making it available, and it has sorting systems and communicative systems allowing everybody to know where they want what information, and where what information can be had, and where there are tasks and working groups which can benefit from each other's knowledge. Knowledge sharing cannot be planned, but we can facilitate knowledge sharing in our organisations and workplaces.

Knowledge sharing is a necessary element in cross-professional problem solving, and knowledge sharing is an essential ingredient in innovation in an organisation.

Innovation

New insight often arises when we cannot get things to fit into our existing understandings and expectations. The spontaneous production of knowledge often happens in situations which activate differences or disagreements, and if such disagreements trigger insecurity, the group and its members will feel an impulse to leave them behind and hurry on, because they feel the ice breaking under their feet. But it does also happen occasionally that reality is allowed to enter when it knocks on the door. Have we not all experienced surfacing from a challenging situation, shaken, wiser and stronger? The trick is to tease out the secrets of such situations and then recreate them. The Chilean biologist Humberto Maturana, who is interested in human cognition, points to three conditions which must be present for people to learn and develop acceptance, just enough disruption, and scope for reflection, in the sense of both mirroring and contemplating. These three conditions must be components in the design of an organisation's 'learning space' (Maturana & Varela, 1987/1992).

We cannot expect knowledge sharing to happen spontaneously. Neither can we expect innovation to happen spontaneously. It takes a professional and managerial effort. Dorthe Thorning, who is managing director of the industrial firm Fiberline Composites, here explains why the company has entered a partnership with artists. It is not difficult to recognise Maturana's three conditions in her description:

"Art has so much to offer: it can be beautiful, decorative, and create an atmosphere. It can provoke and shake us out of our habits and everyday routines. It can ask the basic, perhaps uncomfortable, ethical questions, so we are forced to think. Art can also entertain and make us laugh, and when we are laughing together, we open up and allow some of our barriers to fall. These are all qualities which stimulate openness and promote dialogue."

This is an example of a company which is deliberately inviting different art forms and different artists as partners in order to create space for learning. In the meeting between technicians, engineers and economists on the one side of the borderline, and artists and humanists on the other, tension increases and the creative questioning and stimulation become tangible. But every such encounter between professionals – just a brief exchange between the informatics consultant and the receptionist – carries a similar potential. In order to utilise these dynamics, the organisation must ensure that encounters take place between people who understand themselves and each other as bearers of culture, and who know the importance of culture. The organisation must also ensure that the encounter takes place in a physical environment which awakens curiosity and engagement. It is necessary to arrange space and situations in which energy can be transformed into knowledge and new thinking for the benefit of all. The organisation must develop a common language which will carry the parties onward for information and experiences to flow as freely as possible and to ensure access for all.

Companies like Fiberline, which focus on developing knowledge and innovation, have developed strategies, philosophies and practices for making it possible. Such companies will have organisational space where knowledge is created. This means that the experiences drawn from the production process are translated into knowledge. Forms of meeting and working methods will stimulate creative processes and the sharing of knowledge, that is communication and formulation of knowledge to make it available and useful for others than those who first created it. There will be procedures for assessing and evaluating processes, products and results.

Cross-professional problem solving

Not all companies or workplaces are facing a daily demand for innovation. But there is hardly one workplace where the everyday performance of tasks is not dependent on problems being solved in a cross-professional forum. This was also the case in this children's day care institution, where the staff gained an important experience in seeing themselves as cultural beings. The workplace had hardly more than one profession, the childcare profession, so their cultural autopilot was seldom questioned.

This large institution received 70 children between ages three and twelve every day. When playground and outdoor areas were due for renovation, several professions became involved: landscape gardeners, educational experts, architects, engineers, environment and security people from the local authority. A year and a half later, the head of the institution recalls: "At first this collaboration was difficult. It wasn't so much the fact that we all knew different things and had an understanding of different things – it was rather the style. For example, the others had some entirely different ground rules for planning meetings. We felt we were being steamrollered, and they noticed of course – they probably thought us cross. Then they apologised and explained that it was simply their way of being engaged and efficient – and we did see that really, so the atmosphere changed completely. We may not be the world champions in making decisions and getting started, but we felt the energy it gave... and then there was the point about priorities. We wanted everything looking aesthetically good, and we felt that all those gardening people wanted was for it to be easy to maintain. But have a look! They were right – those tree trunks are incredibly beautiful, and the kids play on them all the time. We wanted living trees with leaves and flower beds, but the gardeners said that we needed something that would function from day one. I'm just so happy that we didn't insist on our dream of flowerbeds right there! ...On the other hand, they said that they were becoming maladjusted from all this contact with teacher types. They felt they had started 'reflecting'... I believe they meant it in a positive way!"

This cross-professional working group did not allow itself to be blocked by cultural differences and disagreements. They turned off their autopilots and developed a good intercultural understanding of each other's different perspectives and ways of approaching a task. They developed an intercultural engagement – an appetite for each other and willingness to learn from each other – and they developed a language which enabled them to reach each other. The head's story is that of a professional partnership which went beyond integrating the natures of the different professions to integrate their cultural dimensions too.

When encounters fail

The success of a cross-professional encounter depends on the participants' ability to use their cultural intelligence. If this condition is absent, the risk is high that the encounter at the boundary line will trigger fright and professional dizziness – it feels as if there is a chasm or as if chaos is reigning on the other side of the line. There is a risk that the encounter will release irritation and 'cultural offence'.

Defence mechanisms will show themselves in resistance in the form of tugs-of-war, flattening of opponents, and all sorts of professional disputes. Another defence mechanism is total withdrawal where all communication is abandoned or surrendering, throwing in the towel and compromising one's own profession.

The professional cultures have proved their right to exist. The routines with which these cultures equip us are, in the most literal sense of the word, a true and tested path which leads us forward in our own profession. When our routines, our ways of thinking, understanding and acting are questioned, it can feel rather uncomfortable, improper or unpleasant, we lose our foothold and feel estranged. A ship's engineer talks of his first time in a cross-professional project group:

> "I had an unpleasant feeling that I was running on my emergency generator, that I was only able to deliver what was absolutely necessary. I wanted to go full steam ahead, but they wanted me to document things. I wasn't used to that at all, and I felt it was a waste of time. For a person like me, it was like treading water. It took some time before I felt on top of things. It wasn't fun – I've always been the one out in front!"

We may often not be aware that it is not merely professions, but people with different cultures who meet. When we are met by technical terms and technical jargon, we realise that we do not understand each other. But when the issue at play is different preconceptions, we are rarely aware that we are talking from different cultural home turfs. The feeling of awkwardness, lack of sense or rejection will then be interpreted as 'bad chemistry, conflicts of interests, or lack of competence'. We may not realise at all that we are facing each other with different perspectives, different interpretations, different preferences and priorities, different languages and different expectations. When marketing people encounter their legal colleagues' demands, reservations and critical questions, they often experience it as having their wings clipped and being harassed. If their cultural intelligences had been better developed, they would have experienced it as their colleagues' contribution to quality control, to ensuring that the company will not be pulled into court. Parameters such as 'skill' and 'professionalism' (professional core values), are assessed very differently in different cultural contexts. Just listen to this account from a salesman in an IT firm who had attended his second meeting with a group of subject heads from a large educational institution.

> "One wonders how they earn their money... no decisions were made as far as I could tell. But they had a lot of good thoughts and a few ideas. But it was all so vague... I really didn't know what to do. It's so easy to get to look aggressive or like a know-it-all there."

It is hard to feel engaged when a cross-professional cultural encounter raises doubts: "Can I really trust them? What are their competences? How can I respect people like them?" Or: "Can I really match them? Will I get a word in here?"

Professional cultures do not always realise it when they meet

Thus differences within an organisation or a cross-professional group do not automatically lead to new thinking and results. The outcome depends on how the group members experience and handle their mutual differences. This was demonstrated by the Danish innovation expert Lotte Darsø in her study of the work of project groups in the pharmaceutical company Novo Nordisk, whose commercial development is entirely dependent on cross-professional and otherwise heterogeneous groups developing new products and new ways of using known products. The study was focused not only on differences in professions, but on differences in general. One of her conclusions was that the condition for synergy being generated within a heterogeneous group is that the members of the group experience that they have both mutual similarities and mutual differences (Lotte Darsø, 2001).

Groups experience of being alike and different

Being alike

	Being alike – not experienced	Being alike – experienced
Difference – not experienced	Superficial relations Working in parallel Boredom A	Security Easy Confluence Avoidance B
Difference – experienced	C On guard Culture shock Conflict Silence	D Dynamics Tensions Tolerance Synergy

(Lotte Darsø: *Innovation in the Making*, 2001)

We are automatically most attracted to people who are like us, and when members of a group find that they have many features in common, working together is smooth and easy, but not much new thinking is generated (B in the figure). If contact between the members of a group is merely superficial, the experience gained is limited, and the various competences are not challenged by the interplay (A). If all the group members experience is their differences, they become tense and guarded towards each other. They lose control and become confused at having to interpret all the different signals received from the others, and the productivity of the group is limited (C). When, on the other hand, the group members experience both their similarities and their differences, dynamic tensions are generated in the group which can lead to both conflicts and creativity on the edge of chaos (D) (Darsø, 2001).

It is thus important to ensure that the group members catch sight of their points of similarity as well as their points of difference, of what they agree on and what they disagree on. This process requires openness and a willingness to make oneself visible, and to play an open hand – and it requires curiosity and a willingness to recognise the inputs of other group members as professional contributions. Members of a working group must also be able to talk about their practices, differences and similarities.

> The exciting thing will be to get managers interested in how people come together to talk about what actually happens in organisations. We need innovative cultures, and innovative cultures cannot be designed in conventional ways. Innovation means a shift in patterns of thought and relationships, which fluctuate and intensify through networks.
>
> Shaw, 2002 quoted from Amtoft and Vestergaard, 2003

Talking about the points we agree on or the areas where we are like each other is rarely a problem. Many groups have a tendency to exaggerate their similarities and blur their differences in the hope of maintaining harmony.

It is a vigorous myth that the mere presence of harmony and consensus promotes results. This is not so, and the technical explanation for this is that harmony and consensus fail to identify the crucial interfaces. A number of studies besides the Novo Nordisk study mentioned above point out that the most productive and most innovative working groups have developed the ability to be open and confrontational as an essential feature of their working cultures. Confrontation should here be understood in the sense of a continuous 'face-to-face' discussion at the interfaces between different – and possibly opposing – views, attitudes and work methods. It is also worth noting here that many of the conflicts experienced in working groups are the result of confrontations which failed to materialise in time.

Different types of collaboration

A cross-professional approach and partnership are mantras in most organisations, and they are expressions of hope and intentions as well as necessity. Inherent in both concepts is also a contrast or a state of tension. Public sector organisations as well as private sector organisations need, on the one hand, to have a strong professional element, including increasing expertise and specialisation in a large number of fields. On the other hand, they also need an organisational structure which ensures efficient work routines, short decision-making chains and efficient utilisation of resources, including team organisation, task flow and decentralisation of power structures. These two needs easily come into conflict when applied. We know the battles and the efforts to balance the dilemma: we try with decentralisation only to return to centralisation – then we try a matrix organisation but return to silos. We change between different ways of organising the dilemma.

Intelligent practice in this context shows itself as robustness and the ability to absorb the dilemma. Culturally intelligent working groups will be able to live with the dilemma – and use the field of tension rather as a dynamo for knowledge sharing and innovation. Another characteristic feature of culturally intelligent working groups is the fact that they do not become locked into a certain way of working together, but are able to change back and forth between different ways depending on the task and the situation.

Most organisations form different types of team, project or matrix structures precisely as a strategy to facilitate this. All experience shows, however, that cultures weigh more heavily than strategies, so culture is the dark horse that must be included in the calculation of risks.

The first step towards a culturally intelligent utilisation of different professional cultures is to become aware that a cross-professional approach and partnership assume many forms, and the most appropriate form is determined by the situation in which the group finds itself. Many theorists and practitioners with an interest in professional partnerships use a tripartite division showing the different forms of professional collaboration in the form of three different flowers:

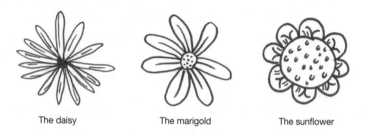

The daisy   The marigold   The sunflower

(Achen, Andersen, Donkin & Hinge, 2003)

If we look at the flowers in turn, each petal represents a professional group which contributes its particular professionalism to the solution of the task. The number of petals in the individual flowers is arbitrarily chosen and does not reflect any particular number of professional groups. The centre of the flower illustrates the cross-professional partnership where the individual professions have dissolved into something else, a kind of meta-professionalism – a common professionalism shaped for this joint task.

The daisy with its many large, separate petals illustrates *multi-professionalism*. The various professional groups are here working next to each other within their strongly separate professional fields. Their engagement is focused on the realisation of the individual profession, and their success depends on the professional performance within the different areas. The various groups are generally organised hierarchically. One professional group can decide the actions of another and take decisions on behalf of the other group. Expertise and services are ordered from across the groups, and communicative efficacy is measured by the degree of friction and flow of such requisitions and deliveries.

The marigold in the middle represents a *cross-professional* approach with focus equally divided between the petals and the centre. The engagement is focused on a joint project and decisions are consensus-oriented. The foundation and the knowledge of the various professional groups are integrated, new knowledge and new attitudes are generated, and shared 'additional knowledge' is created. There is a high degree of professionalism within each professional group, but the participants in the cross-professional partnership represent the total project and not merely the views of their own professional group.

The sunflower is an illustration of a *shared* professional approach where the individual professions are seen as the source and basis of an entirely new shared professionalism. The different professions are therefore less marked, whereas the common core, the integration of professionalisms, is very important. The professional groups which participate in the shared professionalism have a shared knowledge and understanding. A high degree of delegation and a non-hierarchical structure are typical features. There is strong focus on a comprehensive approach – general understanding overrides special interests. The shared responsibility is a central concern. The shared professionalism is recognition and acceptance of the fact that all professional aspects are interconnected. Communication manager Finn Jernø of Fiberline Composites here reports how this belief in a shared professional approach is reflected even in the building design:

> "We wanted a transparent factory where our employees were able to enter into mutual dialogue. Offices and production are separated by glass, so we are in touch with each other and each other's work. We wanted a physical framework which would make people communicate together across the organisation, and where it is evident that we are all part of the same entity."

> The following example shows that the idea of, and ambition regarding, a cross-professional approach can vary quite widely even within the same unit. In answer to the question "What do you actually understand by a cross-professional approach in your area?", one project manager in a drug company said "A cross-professional approach is a partnership of equals from various disciplines or professional groups representing different perspectives and experiences as well as professional competences with the aim of analysing, defining and solving a problem by approaching it from different professional angles".

> In contrast, the project manager's superior places emphasis on the group's shared professionalism when explaining: "Probably the most important thing is to be able to ignore the narrowly professional aspect and be able to enter into cross-wise relations. It probably also takes an element of human curiosity. But the most important element is, I think, the degree of engagement one puts into the shared task".

If the concept of cross-disciplinary collaboration is surrounded by such a state of confusion in a working relationship as close as that of boss and employee, it can have consequences, for example with regard to resource allocation and utilisation in the project group with consequent lack of productivity.

Two essential dimensions

The three types of cross-professional approach can be grouped in relation to two essential dimensions, one of which concerns the role of any specific professionalism in the performance of the task, while the second concerns collaboration across the professional groups.

Professionalism

As described earlier in this chapter, we talk of professionalism as an intersection of profession and function. The element of specific professionalism has a marked presence in multi-professional as well as cross-professional approaches, whereas it is an inherent support structure in an approach based on shared professionalism. In a multi-professional approach, the individual professionalisms are strongly separate, with each team member representing his or her own professional field and setting his or her own goals. The cross-professional approach also contains a strong element of professional awareness, but the individual professional approaches influence each other, and team members have an insight into each other's professions and set their goals together. The outcome is a holistic approach to the work, and the coordination of the various professional approaches. The final product is in principle dependent on all team members making their own professional contributions.

This is not necessarily the case in an approach based on shared professionalism. There is a professional overlap here which means that the task can be performed by various persons, and all professional groups need not contribute their specific professional competences but can stand in for each other.

Differentiation is an absolute necessity for any organisation because it enables employees to specialise, to establish a professional focus, and thus to achieve high professional quality and productivity. But differentiation also has a dark side: it reduces communication between units and makes it difficult to learn from each other. The organisation must therefore develop strategies to promote integration and partnerships. Integration occurs in the form of processes which integrate diverse tasks, functions and professional approaches in a manner which develops synergy, and not competition or downright conflicts within the company.

Collaboration

While this differentiation, in the form of specialisation and the division and delegation of tasks to different professional groups, is moving along, a parallel process is moving in the opposite direction. This is the coordination and integration of the different activities which the company has put into action in order to perform its tasks. This opposite process is absolutely necessary for ensuring that the resources are utilised, and that a comprehensive and coherent approach is developed for the task.

Coordination occurs in the form of collaboration between the various professional groups. Collaboration involves close interplay among the parties involved – they must have a good mutual relationship and see each other as partners and colleagues. Collaboration requires 'team qualities'.

Team qualities depend on the parties having some degree of knowledge of each other and awareness of each other's existence and of the importance of each other's roles in solving the shared task. At one end of the scale we have 'minimum' collaboration with the individual contributions arranged like beads on a string, one following the other. If a bead is missing, the process will stop, and when a colleague has delivered his bead, he withdraws. This linear form of collaboration is what the real estate agent below is referring to: "Just a moment, I'll check that our office assistant has put out the photos, so we can continue…" This situation involves a case of simple coordination of the responsibilities of two professional people. Further up the scale – towards full integration – we meet the diverse group which came together to make a playground for 70 children.

In sum, we note that the concept of a cross-professional approach describes a work situation in which weight is placed on both a high professional level as in a multi-professional approach, while considerable demands are also made on the groups' ability to work together as in the shared professional approach – both elements are, in our view, required for a cross-professional approach.

Professionalism and collaboration are not mutually exclusive, and a cross-professional approach cannot be reduced to being merely an 'in-between' between a multi-professional approach and an approach based on shared professionalism. It is not an 'either-or', but rather a 'both-and' situation, as formulated by this manager of a consultancy firm: "We want our employees to be experts in their own fields so that they can enter into collaboration with others and assist them in developing their fields. We want a high degree of quality in the partnership, and we believe that we'll only be able to achieve that if our employees are at the absolute front edge of their professional fields."

When should the three types of professional collaboration be used?

The different forms of collaboration with their various degrees of cross-professional elements are aligned along a scale which does not have labels reading 'best' at one end and 'worst' at the other. The scale is neutral, expressing no more than differences. The choice and assessment of types of collaboration should depend on the nature of the task, the situation of the organisation, and the ambitions entertained with regard to the cross-professional partnership. In other words, the specific need should be what governs the choice of type of collaboration. The sunflower is an ideal image of a shared professional approach. The daisy represents the other extreme, the multi-professional approach, and the marigold is somewhere in between the other two.

A middle manager in a food company explains:

> "There is no question that the sunflower is my ideal of a cross-professional partnership, although it is quite unrealistic to believe that we can get anywhere near this ideal in the near future. I would really be satisfied if only we could do a little knowledge sharing across the borders."

Nevertheless, considerations as to the best option easily end in a ranking, with multi-professionalism (the daisy) being placed on the lowest rung of the ladder and shared professionalism (the sunflower) being seen as the highest obtainable form of professional partnership. This is a common view among managerial staff. The tendency to rank the different types does, however, tend to reflect a need for keeping group members or company employees in step, rather than any actual need for knowledge sharing and innovation. If a ranking must be attempted, it should rather be cross-professionalism (the marigold) – in its pure form – that is given the top score, as it has a strong focus on both professionalism and partnership. But in a situation where everything depends on short term bottom-line results, most will probably prefer a work structure tending towards multi-professionalism:

> For instance, it's not easy to take time off from the primary activity – working with clients – for developing partnerships. It's not directly 'productive' work, at least not in the short term, and it can be difficult to consider the time spent as an 'investment' because the benefits are highly uncertain.
>
> Lauvås & Lauvås, 1998

On the other hand, a multi-professional approach can be the expression of an intelligent strategy. Here follows an example where moving from 'sunflower' to 'daisy' makes good sense:

> A big IT company with several different professional groups – engineers, designers, and programmers – had developed a shared professional practice and culture (the sunflower). All played a role in all tasks and all shared largely in the common agenda and the common language. All knew a little of everything and considered themselves as team players rather than as experts within a profession. Then the market changed, and with it the customer base. The demand was now for specialised products for

project management in building and construction and in TV productions, for pig-feeding systems and for adjusting bus and train timetables. Consequently, specialist knowledge of the building industry, the media world, farming and public transport was required. The company's strategy was to change to a multi-professional collaborative work form (the daisy), and this change turned out to require a high degree of professional cultural intelligence among both management and employees.

If, on the other hand, a more flexible, more innovative and less hierarchical structure is desirable, a work form tending rather towards shared professionalism will probably be preferred, as this head of an accounting firm points out: "If we are to survive in the market, we cannot afford any snobbery with regard to functions and levels. Nobody can afford to be exclusive. It is purely the task in hand and the client's needs which count. We simply have to include all good hands to establish a mix to fit the situation. And we have to be able to put up the best team for the job at once, and every time."

The closely coordinated and integrated partnership is stressed in both the cross-professional and the shared professional approaches. Both types place focus on delegation and consensus in decision-making. An essential point is the delegation of responsibility. In a multi-professional approach, responsibility is an individual engagement, whereas shared responsibility, the practical commitment – to both the task and the team – is a characteristic feature of both cross-professionalism and shared professionalism. It happens quite often that this commitment fails to emerge because the cultural intelligence has not been developed in step with strategies and goals. It then happens that projects which were intended and organised as shared professional initiatives with the aim of producing creative innovation remain multi-professional. The parties involved become each other's suppliers and not close partners, as happened in the case below:

> The consultancy firm had worked for some time, focusing on the development of a series of basic principles such as mobility, flexibility and knowledge sharing among its professional experts. The vision was an entirely new, innovative and manoeuvrable company. The problem was that this vision was not followed up. The company was organised into separate business areas, and a system was introduced for registering individual tasks and rewarding individual performances. In a glaring discrepancy from its vision and principles, the firm found itself stimulating not only multi-professionalism but also internal competition.

All talk of what will be the best form of professional collaboration must necessarily be based on the nature of the task in hand, the conditions under which it must be solved, and the people engaged in its solution. When we classify the different forms of professional collaboration in advance, we divert attention from the system which the cross-professional approach is to serve.

It is worth noting that all three flowers focus on professionalism, but they understand professionalism differently, and the coordination of the various professions is different. True cross-professionalism in our sense finds expression first and foremost in the ability to move smoothly from one form to another as the situation demands.

The inherent tension field of cross-professionalism

We rarely see the three types of professional collaboration in their pure form in the practical world. A more likely situation is various possible combinations between focus on 'professionalism' and focus on 'collaboration'. Indications are that cross-professionalism in its pure form is a state rarely occurring and highly unstable.

Those who participate in a cross-professional partnership must keep a two-dimensional focus at all times – on the individual professionalism and on the shared collaboration. These two foci – which represent differentiation and integration respectively – have a tendency to pull in opposite directions. The state of tension which is a consequence of this dual focus is experienced as an inherent and insoluble paradox. Allocation and specialisation are basic organisational principles, but so is collaboration with other partners, and this brings up the question of integration. How do colleagues, departments and companies coordinate and integrate mutually interdependent activities? Is it the case that a high degree of specialisation inevitably undermines the ability to collaborate and the ability to share a common goal and a common vision for the organisation?

The answer to this question may well be a 'yes' in the practical world, and if the paradox described above is transferred to a cross-professional approach, a pressure away from cross-professionalism towards one of the other two types of professional collaborations may arise.

The paradox is illustrated in the model below.

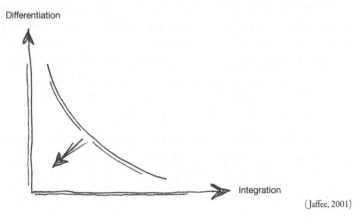

(Jaffee, 2001)

The paradox consists in a kind of symbiosis in reverse, where two desirable and mutually reinforcing states develop a negative or reverse relationship. When the two dimensions of cross-professionalism are plotted into the chart above, it means that as the focus on professionalism is increased, the focus on partnership will decrease – and vice versa.

How then do we wriggle out of this paradox and allow different professions to become each other's support? The answer is that by using our cultural intelligence, we can realise a constructive way of bringing different professionalisms into play.

Three different activities are required for solving the main problem

We have now reviewed different ways in which professionalisms can interact. So far we have referred to processes in the workplace in general, as if the same thing is going on all the time, which it does not. In this section we will demonstrate that professional collaboration takes place in relation to three main types of task, and we show how these tasks can influence the priority given to the various forms of collaboration.

Professionalisms meet and unfold in various types of situation. For the sake of clarity we here take the liberty of simplifying the endless variety of tasks, events and situations. We bundle them into three arenas which are different in nature but mutually connected and interdependent. Each arena obeys its own logic and has its own time perspective. Each one calls for its own special activities and special type of dialogue subject to its own special type of communication, language and agenda (E.L. Dale, 1999).

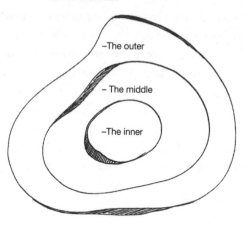

The three arenas

- The outer
- The middle
- The inner

The outer arena is where the practical work takes place – meeting the customer who is asking for a product which is no longer made, or installation of a gas boiler, conversion of a housing loan or treatment of a patient. The outer arena faces the surrounding world. This is where we interface with customers, users and external partners.

The middle arena is where the planning and organisation of activities take place – it may be sorting out stores, meeting other tradesmen on the building site, preparing a team in the bank, or planning the roster in a hospital ward.

The inner arena is where the organisation's think-tank function is placed. This is where we reflect upon the most recent developments in the industry at the six-monthly seminar, or where a challenging relationship with one of the bank's business clients is evaluated, or where lessons are drawn and new thinking developed in relation to a potential new treatment method.

We see all three ways of practising professional collaboration (the flowers) within all the three arenas. When meeting the outside world we sometimes apply our specialist roles to which our education and training give us access, the daisy state. When entering the inner arena, professionalism then dissolves. This is where the service staff and the economist may have some important observations and thoughts which have less to do with their function than with their participation in the shared professionalism. In other situations, for example company consultants visiting a customer they will work across their respective professionalisms and act as generalists, but when developing strategy and new business areas (back in their own office) they use more of their specialist background from economy, marketing and sociology.

The flowers and the three arenas are a way of sorting and a way of taking one's bearing in type, degree, time and place. The models can thus be used as an element in our understanding of cultural intelligence. Let us now look at the various possibilities we have for stimulating the development of professional cultural intelligence in the workplace.

Cultural intelligence in professional cultural encounters

In a culturally intelligent workplace, cross-professional collaboration is more than an intention and more than a technical discipline. It is a daily practice through which professionalism and collaboration are integrated, leading to better quality in problem solving and organisational development. What does it take to make professional cultural encounters constructive and yield results which exceed the sum of the individual professionalities?

A workplace which works in a culturally intelligent manner with cultural professional differences can be recognised on the following features:

- A general awareness that professional cultures are something other and more than competences and eccentricities – and the ability to distinguish between the nature of a profession and its culture.
- Actual commercial and practical needs are the guidelines for determining the manner in which to collaborate.
- A general awareness of the balance between professional integration and professional differentiation.
- A general awareness of the different types of collaboration and a general ability to change back and forth between them.
- A shared awareness that different collaboration approaches are needed within the three arenas, and that there is a synergy between them.
- A shared language, shared agendas and 'space' for dialogue have been developed in all three arenas.
- A clear shared idea of what makes an intelligent encounter of different professional cultures in the workplace, with the result that everybody is able to feel and recognise intelligent practice as well as less-intelligent practices in himself and in others.

When it becomes necessary to switch off the cultural autopilot and move into manual control, it is necessary to think in terms of 'manual facilitation'. This is because it is impossible to steer one's way to either cross-professionalism, innovation or cultural intelligence. But it is possible to facilitate them. Facilitation means first and foremost to allow for the need of professional people to find a professional foothold. This can be done by putting down stepping stones and sighting points in the uncertain and impenetrable no-man's land between the professional groups.

The last part of this chapter will present four methods for putting down stepping stones and establishing sighting points in situations where the intention is to bring different professionalisms into play with and against each other for cross-professional problem solving, the sharing of knowledge or innovation.

Creating clarity

A starting point for the development of cultural intelligence in an organisation is to raise the general awareness of the implications of the presence of different professional cultures. This includes clarifying the actual situation and need for collaboration, and deciding what role the professional cultures should play in this context as well as when and how they should confront each other. In this way the CI development is initiated through the cognitive dimension, cultural understanding.

As we have seen, the members of a working group move in and out of the three different arenas, and the manner in which they move between the arenas decides whether the professional rationality will be generated. The boundaries of the three arenas should therefore be made clear so as to ensure that the relevant cross-professional partnership is chosen in the right situation. The three flower figures will help to decide which type suits a given task.

The frameworks and agendas of the different arenas are shown in this matrix which can be used for clarification (inspired by Dale, 1999).

The outer arena

This is about realising the organisation – professional and practical competences are required.

The burning questions are: How do we perform the tasks together? How do we become productive and efficient?

What competences and processes will facilitate this part of the task? Where should the various professionalisms be integrated – and where should they be differentiated? Who has the power to decide? How do we make decisions?

The middle arena

This is about planning the organisation's next step – methods and technical competences are required here.

The burning questions are: How do we organise ourselves? How do we attack the problems?

What competences and processes will facilitate this part of the task? Where should the various professionalisms be integrated – and where should they be differentiated? Who has the power to decide? How do we make decisions?

The inner arena

This is about developing the organisation – creative, critical and visionary competences are required here.

The burning questions are: How do we see ourselves, our surroundings and our work? Where do we want to go?

What competences and processes will facilitate this part of the task? Where should the various professionalisms be integrated – and where should they be differentiated? Who has the power to decide? How do we make decisions?

The cultural propeller

As noted, a group can only work effectively and innovatively if its members are aware of the interfaces between professions and of elements which reach beyond them, such as professional ambition and professional responsibility. A good method of visualising similarities and differences within a group is the 'cultural propeller'.

The propeller illustrates the cultural dynamics which drive the practice of any given professional group – for better or worse. It is important to be aware that the propeller is a method for generating dialogue and not a diagnostic tool (Ofman, 2002).

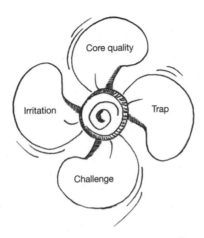

The propeller can be used by two groups to reflect upon their own culture in relation to that of the other group, using their experiences with each other.

The propeller has four blades:

Core quality: This is a style or a talent of ours which has a useful expression. If the core quality is removed from us as a professional group, we would no longer be recognisable.

Trap: This is when we overplay our core quality, when it becomes too much of a good thing – too long, too often, too persistent, too one-sided.

Challenge: This is an ability which we feel we lack at least partly, but which you have as one of your core qualities, and which we admire. It is a challenge to us, something we can learn from you and which will complement and balance our core quality.

Irritation: This is when our challenge is overplayed by the other group, when they do it too long, too often, or too one-sidedly. The positive side of 'irritation' is expressed in the core quality.

Here follows an example of how a group of administrators and technicians filled in the cultural propeller in order to visualise some of the important cultural differences between them.

• The administrators:
Core quality: We administrators wish to be seen as careful and accurate. We take pride in this and we probably expect others to be equally careful.

Trap: The trap is that we overdo it so that we lose ourselves in details and fail to see the whole picture.

Challenge: This is why our challenge is to learn to take a more general and long-term view. We admire that in the others.

Irritation: On the other hand, we hate working with people who get airy-fairy and vague. That's one impression we definitely don't want to give!

• The technicians:
Core quality: We technicians believe that we are practical and focused on finding solutions – that's one of the things we stand for.

Trap: We sometimes get a bit blunt and overlook the finer nuances.

Challenge: Our challenge is probably mainly to learn to stop and think without getting impatient. We're too quick off the mark sometimes!

Irritation: But we hate to dawdle and never get anything done. It's so irritating to deal with dawdlers and inefficiency!

This is the introduction to a shared dialogue on the possibilities for learning from each other and on the risk of tripping up each other and the group's work. It gives the group the opportunity for identifying and absorbing those 'alien' elements which can create learning if invited in. With careful facilitation, this method will not only develop the group members' cultural understanding but also their mutual empathy; it will also generate examples of how to improve multi-professional dialogue in the workplace.

Managing a heterogeneous group

Cultural expert Nancy Adler takes an even more nuanced view of cultural interfaces. Using the model shown below, she points to the fact that an important managerial responsibility is to assist a group of employees in changing focus from differences and disagreements to similarities and agreements, depending on the needs of the moment. How, for example, do we keep a project group united and on track while utilising the energy from their differences and the fractures within the group as the driving force in the project?

This figure illustrates how the group leader's desire to spark off and promote various processes has consequences for her choice of intervention. The figure also shows that different types of task or stages are supported by different processes, and it points to a reflective way of facilitating a group as an alternative to compromises or 'first one way and then the other' that are often the consequences when handling challenging heterogeneity. This model can act as a general framework for the development of all three dimensions of cultural intelligence in a group.

Managing a heterogeneous project group

Stage	Process	Diversity makes the process...	Intervention
Entry: Initial team formation	Trust building (develop cohesion)	More difficult	Using similarities and understanding differences
Work: Problem description and analysis	Ideations (create ideas)	Easier	Using differences
Action: Decision making and implementation	Consensus building (agreeing and acting)	More difficult	Recognising and creating similarities

(Adler, 1997: 140)

Sponsoring culture and cultural features

In situations where we want cross-professional practice to lead to innovation, knowledge sharing and cross-professional problem solving, we must be prepared to reward or 'sponsor' the cross-professional practice which creates these results. If the effort has been made to organise a company into groups and networks, individual measurements and rewards must be abandoned because they work against the strategy.

If management genuinely wants the different professions not only to live peacefully side by side – to keep each other in check, so to speak – but to integrate them to create synergies, it is necessary to support and realise the cultural features which promote constructive encounters between the professions. The aim is not to change attitudes, but to support actions.

When we put energy and effort into the incentive structure, the organisational structures and the organisational communication are changed so as to better stimulate the desired results. We cannot provide support without such structures. We give support to a particular cultural practice or a particular cultural feature by directing our focus on it and communicating in a special manner. This managerial effort is called 'sponsoring'.

Say it out loud
- Direct attention to the element to be supported, so that the focus is clear to everybody. Give it a name so that everybody knows what they are talking about and what it is called.

Formalise and legalise
- Give the cultural practice a recognisable form which is available to everybody. Make it a high-priority activity. Give it the rubber stamp and make it a practical possibility.

Scale up
- This means taking a personal part and making a visible contribution to the activity in question – also if the world championship is way out of reach!

Scale down
- Stop taking part in practices and activities which do not support – or are contrary to – the desired practice or activity.

Enquire
- Follow up, ask for examples of the desired practice and ensure that it is accessible to yourself and others.

Acknowledge

- Show approval and acknowledge it when you meet the desired practice or hear examples of desired activities. Ensure that the good stories are told and spread around. Acknowledgement can also take the form of a more practical reward or a cash bonus.

Evaluate

- Gather up experiences and new knowledge at regular intervals so as to adjust efforts and support, and if required, scale up or down with respect to the ambitions. It is an important quality of evaluations that all participate, that all know the outcome, and that the course is reset together.

Ideally, all who are members of the organisation should act as sponsors. And the process starts with management. A clear and unambiguous sponsorship of cultural practice is one of management's most important tools.

This chapter has argued that cultural intelligence is crucial in the professional field for the development of professional rationality in the knowledge society. Every professional person and every professional group runs the risk of becoming encased within its own competent thinking. This is why the different professionalisms must be confronted with each other. Cultural intelligence in the professional field is about creating fruitful contacts among professionals across – and with the aid of – the professional cultural differences. This will result in the professions not only supporting each other, but also supporting an entirely new type of professionalism.

4/

THE CULTURAL DIMENSIONS OF MERGERS

Cultural differences *per se* are not the cause of problems in mergers, but culture plays a considerable and varied role in the merging process...

The first part of this chapter deals with the importance of culture and cultural differences in the context of various organisational interweavings, such as mergers and acquisitions. For ease of reference, the various types are dealt with here under one category, as mergers. The latter part of the chapter discusses how to utilise cultural intelligence to achieve a constructive merger process.

When the blame is placed on culture

"Practically all articles, books and reports point to cultural differences as one of the main causes of problems in achieving the anticipated benefits from mergers", the Danish business journalist Per Thygesen Poulsen concluded after his review of the extensive international literature of recent years on mergers. The question is, however, what is here meant by 'culture' and 'cultural differences', and what is the role ascribed to culture in the studies?

Merger problems can take the form of problems of collaboration, a fall in productivity, the resignation of key employees, slow decision-making processes, and a failure to create synergy and harness efficiency from cross-merger projects. The problems can arise in the changeover phase as well as during consolidation. Merger studies often explain such problems by reference to cultural conflicts between the merging organisations. The studies are based on the descriptive definition of culture, which sees culture and cultural differences as a set of features which characterise the organisation and its employees. Seen in light of this definition, the successful merger depends on management's ability to control the cultural differences and build up a strong common culture supported by the employees. If management is successful, the merger will have the desired results. This view, however, sees events as linearly connected, and an organisation as a combination of individual elements which can be combined into a new whole without the elements changing in character. The studies view culture as a variable to be manipulated in the organisation on a par with structure, work tasks, players and technology.

If, on the other hand, we apply the complex understanding of culture and look at culture as a process, the successful merger is one where the employees have created constructive shared cultural traits in the new organisation. These cultures aid the achievement of good results and they are recreated and adjusted by the employees via their collaboration. As the Norwegian organisation consultant Stein Kleppestø emphasises, cultural differences don't create problems in mergers, but they can serve as a convenient excuse when disagreements and problems arise.

The word 'culture' is used in these studies as a metaphor for different organisational phenomena which typically emerge in connection with mergers. A merger will always involve varying degrees of disagreements and power struggles among the managements and employees involved regarding interests, prestige, power, resources and future directions. When problems arise during the merger process, differences in interests and disagreements can prevent the parties from establishing mutual understanding. As the creation of shared meaning and mutual understanding are the first steps in the construction of a shared culture, the constructive culture-creation process will grind to a halt. Or the new cultures which are constructed will tacitly accept power struggles and mutual disagreements, and this will have negative consequences for mutual collaboration and performance. We seek the company of those who agree with us and position ourselves in opposition to those with whom we disagree, and cultural differences are then used in explanation. "It's because the others are so bent on centralising and can't look further than procedures – procedures!" "It's probably because we come from a management culture which is more democratic than theirs." "Our cultures are far too different."

To call disagreements cultural differences is a way of disclaiming responsibility, and culture is here used simply as an excuse for not looking beyond the surface. The reference to cultural differences is an effective 'showstopper', signalling as it does some fundamental value conflicts for which the individuals involved refuse to take responsibility, or feel they can't change. The point is that it is necessary for us to focus on what lies behind the problems and admit that conflicts of interest and disagreements are involved, and that they must be dealt with by us all together.

Cultural differences *per se* are not the cause of problems in mergers, but culture plays a considerable and varied role in the merging process by the sheer fact that a merger represents a process of extensive cultural integration – the joining of several wholes, each with its own cultural pattern, into one new whole. The shared constructive creation of a new culture is the foundation on which mutual understanding must be built and a precondition for preventing problems in the numerous cultural encounters which make up a merger process.

An organisation's cultures

The elements which make up the strongest ingredients in the melting pot of a merger are the different organisational cultures, and they take their features from a company's trade, its national cultures and its special characteristics. The particular workplace culture of an organisation develops throughout its history, being formed by those who have worked there, by their successes and struggles, by top figures, by accidents, and by experiences reaped from particular events. The organisation itself and everybody within it have acted and reacted in response to different situations, and this has gradually created a pattern. Some cultural features can be changed quickly, as when everybody started arriving at meetings on time because the new boss started the meetings on time. It would not have had the same effect if it had been the new office trainee who had cleared her throat when the clock struck, for culture is influenced by power relations.

Organisational cultures are rarely a unified culture, as an organisation will comprise various cultures depending on factors such as fields of work, geography, and the persons involved. There will be clear cultural differences between R&D, accounts, marketing and production because the different units perform different roles in the organisation, and their self-awareness differs accordingly. Often they define themselves in contrast to each other even if simultaneously seeing themselves as all part of the same organisation and the wider organisational community. Moreover, the organisation's employees will all have different cultural affiliations – age, ethnic background, gender and nationality – and these differences will also colour the organisation's cultural features.

When speaking about an organisation's culture, we are speaking about a collective perception of a unifying whole, a perception which is clearest when seen in relation to other organisations in the outside world. It is made up of the stories which the employees tell about themselves. The perception of a shared culture is, however, mainly centred on shared values and goals, for as the American organisational psychologist Joanne Martin points out, it is difficult to get consensus on cultural features across different hierarchical positions and functions. Only a small part of an organisation's cultural features comprises elements which everybody sees and on which everybody agrees. It is necessary to accept that many cultural features within the organisation are mutually contradictory, ambiguous and undergoing constant change. There can be inconsistencies between what is said and what is done, unresolved conflicts between groups, and uncertainty about what goals and values really mean. As Martin puts it, management has no choice but to accept that the organisation is full of complexity and unresolved paradoxes and dilemmas. Oversimplified theories offer management the hope that the development of a strong shared culture will lead to higher productivity and better results; but this is pure wishful thinking and is based on a different understanding of culture than the one offered here.

The teeming sea of diverse cultural features within an organisation exerts considerable influence on results, just as it is true to say that culture is the method used by employees to achieve their results. Cultural traits imbedded in methods of solving problems, answering the telephone, making decisions and providing service to the external world are highly important in contacts with clients and partners, and they are an important part of the total value chain leading to the results. Particular meeting styles, open doors/closed doors, managerial styles, feedback methods, atmosphere and attention to each other's areas influence knowledge sharing, and thus the organisation's ability to develop and think in new ways. Cultural features in the form of certain forms of greeting, dress code, openness, gift schemes, the allocation and fitting up of rooms, lunch habits and coffee and fruit schemes may not be directly associated with the organisation's results, but they can have an indirect influence on them. They signal a sense of community and they can make the employees feel at home and happy – or not so happy – and they can signal various standards such as economy or pampering.

It is thus not only the different organisational monocultures that meet in a merger. The IT department, finance and other professional fields will also share certain features across organisations. New structures and working groups also result in new combinations of professions, ages and genders, and perhaps nationalities. It is thus a multiplicity of group affiliations and self-awarenesses, of similarities and differences that meet each other in a merger process.

Different backdrops for mergers

In Danish, the word for merger is *fusion*. The word *fusion* is used in physics about processes where atoms fuse together and energy is released. One example is the sun, where hydrogen atoms fuse to form helium atoms, releasing a large amount of energy. We may well compare a merger with this fusion process, for as synergy is the hope underlying most mergers, the merger of one plus one should not simply make one, but a whole lot more. The intention is to release energy and to shape this energy into something new and better than before. The new context will provide new work constellations and inspire employees to take another step forward, to take shortcuts and to try out new things.

Mergers are many things, and they differ as to how many employees are affected, and how deeply. A merger may involve the transfer of part of one organisation to another organisation and its integration into the latter, or the collapse of two units into one within the same organisation. When entire companies merge, it may involve the integration of the two main offices with all staff, while the rest of the companies continue practically without change, but with a new shared 'hat'. The studies done by the Danish management researchers Molin and Pedersen show that mergers in private companies typically involve at least the integration of administrative systems, IT systems, staff policies, internal communication and structural change.

Even for employees working in a local production unit, a sales office or a local institution far from the merging units, the process of integration can affect the frameworks within which they are working. "Why do we have to provide such details now in our reports to Finance? Don't they trust us any more?" "Why can't I have a day off to move house any more? That's really mean of management!" Local units are also confronted by the fact that different cultures are at play.

The degree of cultural integration required in any individual merger depends on what, and how much, is merged. This chapter deals with mergers where essential elements are integrated, where the parties involved all have some degree of influence, and where synergy is the goal.

The background to a merger will naturally affect the merger process. There is a difference between acquisitions where one party has the controlling influence and a merger between more or less equal parties. There is a difference between a hostile takeover and a bailout, and between the mergers of related companies which complement each other, or between 'identical' companies where the aim is savings on large-scale operations. Where did the initiative for the merger come from? In a major reform of the public sector in Denmark in 2007, 271 local authorities were reduced to 98 and the initiative for these mergers came from the outside, from the Danish parliament which passed a resolution to the effect that the local authorities were to merge. After this initial step, it was geography and local politics which decided who merged with whom. The background to a merger can give an organisation a strong headwind or a gentle tailwind in its efforts to integrate and create a shared constructive culture during the merger process.

Merger – a process of change in which culture counts

Whatever kind of merger is involved, the significance of culture changes and becomes more important for the employees than it was before the merger was mentioned.

> "Never have we been as aware of our own corporate culture as when it was decided that we were to merge with [company X]. We'd practically taken it for granted until then. But suddenly people began to talk about our special working methods and 'spirit', and how annoying it was that we had to abandon it all now."

Mergers heighten awareness of the corporate cultures and make them visible. When previously independent units have to get together in a new shared unit, employees become very aware of what they must now say goodbye to. Before the merger, their attention was directed at the company's internal interfaces and differences between, for example, production workers, research and development staff and bookkeepers. The elements which held the company together were often not appreciated, such as history, logo, products and name, but the prospect of a merger will shift attention to what is shared and to the interface with the culturally different 'them'. A merger places different topics on the agenda: for example, independence or its opposite, the familiar against the alien. Awarenesses and conversations change, and the company culture gains a new importance for the employees.

Major organisational processes of change are all about 'saying goodbye to all that's old and familiar and learning new things'. This applies whether the process concerns the introduction of a new IT system or changes to structures or the physical framework. Here too the organisation's culture plays a role insofar as such changes can mean that work methods, partnership relations and self-awareness have to be renegotiated. In a merger, the process is more dramatic, as a merger involves an inbuilt conflict with one or more other units, a conflict which is about existence and future opportunities. Typically, we have to dissolve our own unit and integrate with others, and the merger implies a potential battle between previously independent units on how the new shared unit should be organised. Who decides what, and who will set their stamp on what?

> Even when production and products are almost identical, the cultural differences between two merging partners can be considerable. Two high-tech companies were merging. In one, all work was carefully planned and monitored, engineers and controllers had considerable power, and management focused solely on whether the results matched the targets. The second partner was a family-owned company where decisions were made subjectively, and where creative product development was a major goal. The culture was strongly business- and service-oriented. The company reacted quickly, and the customer had the last word. Consequently, long-term planning and follow-up were not important. Both companies were successful, so each had reason to feel that its method was the right way of organising a business. The merger between them required a long process of finding shared goals and getting in step before the integration of the two employee groups could commence.

The merger process – if successful – is a process of transformation in which the merging parties are smelted and reshaped in a new mould. The employees must leave one culture and become co-creators of new cultural features in the shared organisation.

Merging processes are one of the biggest challenges facing organisations today. An ever-increasing number of processes of change in organisations involve mergers, and cross-border amalgamations and affiliations are a way of taking expedient action in the public as well as the private sector, at home and abroad.

Marriage with the neighbour or the enemy

People's own culture becomes particularly important in situations where previous competitors in the same market merge. It may then feel as if they are asked to marry the enemy. For years they have fought for the same customers, watched each other's games, and imitated moves and countermoves aimed at retaking market shares or taking the lead once and for all. In a situation such as this, it is something of a challenge to suddenly have to cooperate for the common good.

> "I think it would be much easier if we could merge with a local authority on Zealand, for we have rather too many opinions about our next door colleagues, and that makes working together difficult." This was the thought of a Danish executive in autumn 2005 when his own and the neighbouring local authorities had begun the merging process.

Mergers in the recent Danish public-sector reform took place between neighbouring municipal districts which had lived side by side for a long time with varying degrees of collaboration or the lack of it. Each district had built up an identity and a self-awareness over the years which was based on how they felt they were better than and different from their neighbours: "X-borough is a rural municipality where we're close to the residents and the politicians. We have an informal style and we work well together with all parties because we know each other so well." (Meaning: our big neighbour

Y-borough is top-heavy and bureaucratic). "In Y-borough we have a well-oiled organisation with clear competences. We are a modern city authority, and we work professionally with the business community." (Meaning: X-borough is a tiny rural municipality where they work like one big family and don't have the resources for keeping up to date in all professional fields).

Whether or not the bridegroom is the neighbour or the enemy, the parties know each other and are part of each other's self-awareness – consciously or unconsciously. The employees will have pronounced preconceptions about the others, and part of the organisation's identity is composed of points where they differ from the others. These aspects of the organisational culture will be strengthened when a merger is in prospect, and they can generate sparks in the merger process.

The cultural integration starts before we think – and is more important than we think

A simple three-phase model for the merging process is: before the merger, changeover/implementation, and consolidation. The phase length will vary from merger to merger, and so will the way in which the process moves from phase to phase, but it is true to say in general that it starts before management suspects it and it can take years before it subsides.

Private companies and public organisations operate under different conditions. Mergers in the private sector are generally not published until planning has started and the top management is in place, while the Danish public-sector reform provides an example of the time lapse (two and a half years) in the public sector from publication of the suggestion of a merger until the concrete decisions and implementation processes begin in the new units. Timing and speed will set an important condition for the merger process. A merger involves various integration processes and they generally follow a pattern as shown in the figure below.

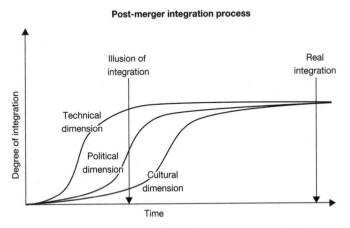

Post-merger integration process

(Inter Cultural Management Associates, Konsulentmateriale)

At the start of the merger process, the organisation's management is totally absorbed in the 'technical aspects' such as finances, legal issues and organisational structure. Next up are the organisation's policy decisions on how to allocate power, who is to have what position, what will happen, what should be done about logo, name and information systems, and who should be placed in which buildings and offices. When these things are decided, management may succumb to the illusion that the merger is largely in place and that the rest will follow along the way. "We have explained why the merger is important and planned what to do; now all we need is to get it done." But this is wishful thinking with eyes closed to the cultural dimensions of a merger, and it will lead to problems.

Culture will be on the agenda right from the start of the merger. Working groups across the merging organisations prepare the concrete integration, this work brings the cultural differences to light, and they will be felt in major as well as minor issues. Then, when the plans are to be implemented in the new units, the employees must break old habits and work routines, take leave of former colleagues and enter into new partnership constellations. Nevertheless, many studies show that the cultural dimension is often assigned next to no, or a highly subordinate, role in the planning of the merger strategy. Management will fail in its duties if it underestimates the importance of providing professional guidance in the daily practical partnerships where people with different cultural backgrounds meet each other.

New cultures will emerge in the merged organisation under all circumstances. The behavioural ground rules for the new organisation will develop in response to different events, strong personalities and concealed and open power struggles. But these ground rules may not be constructive. If a culture has been allowed to form around power struggles, extra effort will have to be put in to clear up misunderstandings and regenerate trust.

Management's creation of culture is watched through a magnifying glass

The very manner in which the merger process is planned is an important part of the new cultural features, and it will have a considerable influence on the success of the merger process because it is itself a process of creation in which new cultures are born – consciously or subconsciously. The planning sets the scene for more than itself, and there is no such thing as a neutral strategy or rational planning. Everything will have a bearing on the inter-human processes, and a professional focus must be placed on the desired cultural dimensions and cultural features to be promoted in the new organisation.

Top management in a large newly merged organisation wanted to make a serious effort at cultural bridging, and started with a cultural survey of the organisations to be merged. When the results were ready, management spent some considerable time discussing differences and similarities among the cultures and on devising the most effective approach to cultural integration. Middle management and employees had contributed to the cultural survey, and they were wondering why top management was silent. All sorts of interpretations, tales and fantasies about what the bosses were planning now arose during the waiting period. Whereas top management had taken the cultural dimension seriously and saw itself as professional and careful, middle management and employees felt management to be secretive, centralistic and not listening. The result was problems in the ongoing merger process as the employees' trust in management was damaged and they were on their guard.

The cultural transformation starts earlier than one would think, and to this should be added the fact that top management often underestimates the signalling value of its own actions, statements and decisions. Management practice is constantly in focus among middle management and employees. Members of management are role models, and whatever they say or do – or do not say or do – will be interpreted as an expression of the new culture. It spells disaster for the merging process if words and action do not match. Nice words will become a boomerang for management if contradicted by their everyday actions. Interpretations commence as soon as the first signals about the merger appear. What is said, how and by whom? What is not said? Why is it always X who is speaking about the merger? Why are the organisations mentioned in that order? Why is nothing said about staff reductions? Which words are being used?

Some managers and consultants use a traditional crisis psychology model for explaining employees' psychological reactions to mergers and other major changeover processes. According to this model, a person will pass through the following phases: shock, reaction, processing, and new directions. A merger will always involve a goodbye, and it is a good idea to signal that psychological reactions and problems may be experienced, but the model offers a far too simple picture of the reactions. A merger also involves positive opportunities, and besides, no two people are the same. Some will not experience any crisis, but will be looking forward to new colleagues and new contexts.

The expression 'resistance to change' describes another unproductive approach to the creation of a merger culture. Employees' critical questions, passivity, complaints, tardiness and objections make some managers react by saying "The employees are not doing what I tell them. They resist change." When talking with employees, we find, however, that only a small part of this is about conscious obstruction. From their point of view, there is a need for clarity, grief at the breaking up of office partnerships and saying goodbye to the workplace, and dissatisfaction at not being involved. The manager calls the reactions 'resistance' because they are in the way of the easy implementation of strategies and plans; but to do so turns the merger into a fight between manager and employees.

An alternative is to call the reactions 'sadness' and 'growing pains', where the sadness is about the inescapable goodbye to something which will never return, and the growing pains are about the effort to find one's place in the new organisation, and perhaps the challenge of handling new tasks. The adoption of this terminology offers a different interpretation and admits other methods of tackling negative reactions. Furthermore, it will influence the merger culture in the direction of the attitude that it is natural to react, that it is a transitional phase, and that ways must be found to establish an organisational cold frame where the tender new shoots can put down roots, and where new and constructive cultural features can grow and develop.

Synergy from complexity

A merger is by definition a complex situation, and its result cannot be predicted or subjected to detailed planning. If the attempt is made to put all details in place in advance, the result will be some rash decisions and far too simple solutions which will prevent the generation of synergy. There must be scope for revising the plans gradually as the integration process unfolds, as potential benefits and unexpected results lie waiting out there in the uncertainty. Determinism, understood as a lack of ability to change plans, is a direct obstacle to the successful merger implementation if the desired results include increased knowledge sharing, learning and synergy. This is the result of the extensive literary review carried out by the organisation researchers Anne-Marie Søderberg and Eero Vaara.

The British organisation researcher Ralph Stacey's matrix illustrating complexity in an organisation can aid our understanding of the merger process and of the forces required for the release of new energy. The matrix also provides an insight into why the temptation often arises to oversimplify explanations and methods.

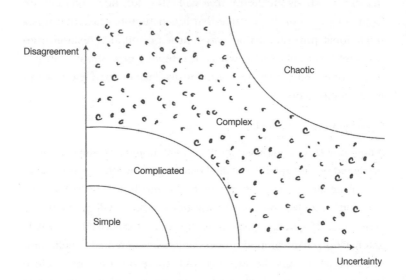

A more complex reality

Disagreement

Chaotic

Complex

Complicated

Simple

Uncertainty

The matrix introduces two dimensions, the degree of uncertainty and the degree of agreement, where agreement/disagreement applies to understanding, experience and views.

The simple field provides scope for planning and comparison with previous experience, and the aim is to repeat what has already proved to be effective in the past. If the situation turns complicated by an increase in uncertainty, detailed planning is no longer possible as it was in the simple field, and it becomes necessary to formulate a mission or vision to provide a general direction for the organisation. If, on the other hand, the complication is caused primarily by growing disagreement, it becomes necessary to negotiate a solution, but it may also be uncertainty and disagreement together which make the situation complicated. Most management literature and most management theories and methods deal with problems in the simple and complicated fields of the matrix.

In principle, however, a merger process falls within the complex field. The complexity may be caused by strong disagreement on well-known factors, or – despite solid agreement – by heavy uncertainty about what is happening, because the organisational course is set for the unknown. Complexity may also arise from disagreement and uncertainty together. Although it may be possible to draw on experience from previous mergers, each new merger will constitute an entirely new challenge.

The model should be seen as dynamic. A merger starts by being complex just as new ideas and new initiatives are, but during the planning and implementation process, things become clearer and they no longer appear so full of contradictions and uncertainty. Some processes move more swiftly than others and decisions are gradually implemented, early results are followed up, management and employees fill in the frameworks, and things quieten down in the new surroundings. Everybody learns to handle the new situation. Things suddenly feel familiar again and nobody can remember how challenging things used to be. But the various processes do not move at the same time or in parallel throughout the organisation. Some can have stabilised, while others are close to chaos. The ability to contain and handle this lack of synchronism is a major part of professional merger management.

While complexity is a condition which can be turned to advantage, the model's chaos field indicates an unhealthy state. Stacey's point is that creativity, innovation and the break with traditional ways of doing things happen in the complex field, and that a variety of managerial approaches is required in order to handle the multifaceted situation. Traditional management approaches are inadequate in the complex field because they are based on an idea of controllability and rationality, and thus impede new thinking and innovative constellations. The problem is, however, that it is precisely these approaches which most managers have been trained in. Quality management systems, competence development plans, Balanced Score Card – all presuppose a position in the simple or the complicated zone, while both language and approaches are lacking for leadership in the complex zone. Many managers therefore retreat from the complex zone with its uncertainty and openly problematic issues which are impossible to control. Managements meet big and contrary demands from owners in the complex zone, as owners – be it in the public or the private sector – want certainty and measurability on the one hand, while on the other demanding innovation and synergy.

Cultural differences meet in the complex zone

A successful merger thus depends on management's ability to lead in the field of complexity so that the organisation benefits from the renewed energy which is released by the merger, while gradually also being able to lead the employees on to hard ground so that the merger is implemented and changes into a new and better working day. Where, then, do the cultural aspects of the merger come into play?

It is precisely the encounter between cultural differences which is the precondition for the merger's leading to synergy and interesting results. Cultural diversity represents different perspectives depending on education, experience, attitudes and personalities which are confronted with each other in the merger. A merger may be compared with a journey in which everybody leaves their usual bases to travel together into the unknown in order to create something new. It follows that the aim should not be to cause as little disruption for management and employees as possible, but to create 'appropriate disruptions' which can generate energy and new thinking. This happens in practical terms via numerous small situations, dialogues and meetings. This is where a lot of people create the new organisation within the framework which the merger management has set. It happens in planned and spontaneous situations, small and large, face-to-face meetings and via the telephone, writing and reading. These are tools by which thousands of relations and cultural encounters are established, and through which the process is shaped and interpreted. This is why the merger process plan must provide scope for constructive disruptions, spontaneous cultural encounters and reflections on the complex situation.

A merger is an obvious opportunity for dropping unsuitable work routines and partnership constellations which have become too fixed. Groups and organisational units have a tendency to repeat themselves and to develop patterns set in fixed moulds on the consensus that the best idea is for things to continue as they have always been. We tend to handle our busy workday by finding our place in our usual roles and in the usual informal hierarchy. We use the methods which usually work and we defend our usual routines by arguing that it is the easiest way. "If it ain't broke, don't fix it". In a situation of relative stagnation, a group's shared culture can act like a lever for change, and a merger can be a gift in that situation because it creates turbulence and the breaking up of petrified patterns.

Many books on mergers focus on organisational cultural differences in mergers as a barrier to integration, and this view reflects how – if at all – many organisations have approached cultural differences in merger processes. If we turn our focus solely to the organisational cultural differences between merging organisations, we run a strong risk of exaggerating their importance and turning them into a collective truth and a projection screen for all the inter-human misunderstandings and difficulties. The trenches between 'them and us' will be dug deeper; and as long as we feel such collective 'truths' to be relevant, we will continue to fill them with our opinion, as Stein Kleppestø points out. The existence of cultural differences becomes a self-fulfilling prophecy, and the differences can be kept alive long after the merger should have been completed.

> A pharmaceutical company was about to merge with a foreign company, and many of the employees had been part of a merger four years previously, when three Danish companies had amalgamated. The prospect of a new merger made it clear that the old merger had not been quite successful. Practically all employees with a minimum of four years of employment in the company were able to point out who had worked in what company before the earlier merger. It was clear that no strong bond to the new shared organisation had been built at the time, as the cultural differences between the merged companies still held meaning and were an adequate explanation for many of the employees.

Turning a merger into a positive and constructive cultural encounter requires a deliberate and competent approach based on the knowledge that culture is created jointly by numerous players. It is not merely organisational cultures that merger managements should be aware of. Encounters between different professional cultures, generational cultures and any ethnic and national cultures can also be active and influence the process in important ways. Every employee belongs to several different cultural communities, so when two human resources departments merge, they will share some HR professional culture, such as technical language, theories and methods. But the concrete manifestation of the HR professionalism can differ quite considerably between the staffs of the two organisations, coloured as it will be by different HR policies, the departments' previous positions of power, the staff's level of experience and age, their gender, technical systems and work procedures. This means that they will enter the new shared HR department with many different self-awarenesses of what it means to be HR staff. Nobody can predict what interfaces and what unexpected questions and alien responses will trigger new ways of thinking and acting.

Power games

Periods of uncertainty are unavoidable in a merger, and power games centred on major or minor stakes will always be played out. Previously independent organisations are dissolved or sold, so considerable attention will be focused on who decides what, and whose systems will be continued. The intention is most often to take the best from the old organisations, but who decides what is best? What happens when the process proceeds across major size differences between the organisations, or across nationalities? Different principles and bases of comparison will compete, and power games for the right to decide the organisation's policies will be played out until a functional power balance is successfully established in the new organisation.

While it is important to be aware of the power play in the merger process, this awareness can also lead to unhealthy tunnel-vision. An example where this happened is provided by a big Swedish company which had bought out a French company. The Swedes went into the merger with the preconception that the French were probably a bit offended by having been bought out by a company from such a small country. The company language was English, so neither the Swedes nor the French were playing on home turf as far as language went. A problem arose in one of the preparatory working groups, as the French group leader sometimes switched to French in emails prior to the meetings, and also distributed some papers in French. The Swedes reacted strongly, interpreting this as typical French arrogance and as a power game in which the French intended to position themselves better in the mutual communication, and thus gain the upper hand in the group. When, after several misunderstandings, the group finally managed to verbalise the language problem, it was found that the group leader was embarrassed about his poor English. Wanting to express himself with the subtlety that would reflect his thorough preparation and satisfy the new owner regarding his work, he had had to switch to French. Was the power game largely a Swedish mirage? It is difficult to know to what extent the French party contributed to the preconception entertained by the Swedes; but if somebody feels that a power game is being played, then there is a power game afoot in the merger, for the belief itself influences reactions and initiatives.

In some mergers it is clear who decides, either because the merger is a buyout, or because difference in size alone decides who has the upper hand. Depending on how this unequal power balance is handled, it can make the employees from the less powerful organisation feel steamrollered and very uncertain of their future.

With the diagram below, the American culture expert Nancy Adler offers a model for visualising power relations and various strategies for coupling merging organisations.

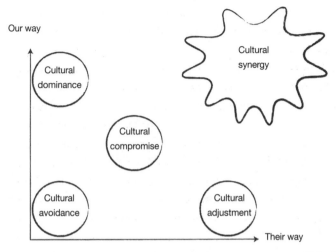

Different strategies

Our way

Cultural synergy

Cultural dominance

Cultural compromise

Cultural avoidance

Cultural adjustment

Their way

(Adler, 1997)

The diagram illustrates the encounter of two different cultures, 'our way' and 'their way', as five different strategies. The merger management must find a balance, but there are no rules of thumb for deciding what position to choose. Compromise and synergy have the most sympathetic ring, but sometimes domination is the most effective approach. However, the poorest strategy is the middle position, the cultural compromise.

Compromise is often the result of management's inability to handle disagreements and cultural differences and the consequent choice of an in-between solution based on existing approaches and systems. In contrast to this, the synergy position is placed entirely outside the two axes to indicate that both parties have left their strongholds and moved together on to a new ground which is different and better than the grounds from where they came. New solutions have been developed which accommodate both cultures, but which manifest themselves in ways which are different from the accustomed ones and which both parties consider to be an improvement.

Different individuals may experience the same solution differently, so that while one party finds the solution to be a cultural compromise, the other party may feel it to be cultural dominance. If that is so, the cultural dialogue has not been successful. One party feels that it has been bending over backwards to accommodate everybody, while the other party feel that the others have merely shuffled their own cards differently. A step which is seen by one party as a neutral and practical standardisation can be seen by the other part as an intolerable demonstration of power.

> One example of such a perceived demonstration of power is provided by the merger or reunification of the two Germanys. In order to standardise and modernise, it was decided to introduce identical traffic lights in Berlin. The dismantling and scrapping of East Berlin traffic lights began in 1994, and out went all the little stop-and-go figures of East Berlin. All traffic signs now had to be the same everywhere in Berlin, and it had to be those from West Berlin as they were technologically the more advanced. But it did not take long before protests against the removal of 'Der Ampelmann' began to be heard, because the scrapping of this little stop-and-go figure became a symbol of West Germany's overwhelming dominance in the reunification process. A protest movement arose to resist this rejection of some of the last symbols of East German daily life, and the politicians could not ignore it. Der Ampelmann returned to some of the Berlin traffic lights.

A merger culture characterised by power struggles, and long-term uncertainty among management and employees, will impair the social working environment and may result in increasing sick leave, dwindling results and key employees leaving the organisation. One way of creating clarity and trust is for management to be clear and honest about which different merging strategies will be used in what situations during the integration process.

Cultural intelligence in merger processes

A merger process must stand on both feet. It must of course have focus on the main issues for the merging companies while at the same time create the best possible frameworks for developing constructive new cultural features. Managers at all levels and employees come from different units and bring their self-awareness and preconceptions about the others into the merger with them. A culturally intelligent merger process requires solid work to get the goal of the merger and the vision for the new organisation to make meaning all the way to the outermost limb of the organisation, so that new constructive cultural features can grow out of the partnership.

It is important to encourage management and employees to adopt a curious and explorative approach to each other's backgrounds, and make them able to adjust expectations and shared ground rules. The ground rules could address management styles, handling of disagreements, decision-making processes, positive and critical feedback, methods of problem solving and the degree of freedom to choose methods. A new common language must be created throughout the new organisation, for words and concepts can no longer be automatically assumed to mean the same.

There are several different models and tools to choose between if we want to work in a culturally intelligent manner in a merger process, and in the following we will present a selection of these and explain how they combine the different dimensions of cultural intelligence. The following approaches are involved:

1. Working strategically with values and culture
2. Exploring culture in preparation for the merger
3. A model for understanding
4. Follow-up on and implementation of cultural traits.

Working strategically with values and culture

In order to create a good framework for the development of constructive cultural features in a merging organisation, we must focus on three elements: vision, values, and ground rules.

The *vision* for the new organisation must establish a clear, necessary and attractive future perspective for the entire organisation in order to ensure that management and employees will be prepared to invest their professional future in it. The vision must promote intercultural engagement in order to motivate management and employees to let go of their old relations and contribute to the building up of new ones. The various cultural backgrounds must not be ignored, but communication must proceed across these differences, and a new shared frame of reference must be generated, and gradually also new cultural features in the various professional fields.

Top management's formulation of the general *values* for the new joint organisation is a good starting point, not only for the creation of the shared culture, but also for the creation of new cultural traits in the various departments. This is because the organisational values constitute the management's general guidelines for constructing the framework within which a good working life can develop in the new organisation, as well as for the manner in which it is desired that people should act towards each other. Top managers cannot steer and control the growth of new cultural features, but they can indicate a direction and some expectations, and they can plan the cultural integration process in a manner that will allow all to contribute and assume responsibility for the creation of culture via many forms of activities and dialogues. There must be room for reflection and uncertainty, and many opportunities must be provided where cultural features can be discussed and adjusted. The creation of a constructive culture can be promoted by increasing the awareness of culture, especially the awareness of how values and culture influence collaboration and results.

The integration process must provide opportunity for translating the general values into purposeful and meaningful ways of collaborating in the workplace. Managements and employees in the individual units must negotiate and agree new cultural practices to match the new situations and to express the general values in various ways.

Formulating *ground rules* for the new partnerships is a good method of turning the general rules into concrete objectives; it also contributes to the attempt to design new cultural traits. Doing so also provides an opportunity for the individual to formulate what he sees as his central qualities and competences, and this in turn will lead to greater mutual understanding of each other's backgrounds and of why we may think and act differently. Ground rules for a partnership create common ground and a sense of security from which a productive partnership can develop to deal with the complexities of the situation.

Formulating the ground rules will improve management's and employees' ability to communicate in a culturally intelligent manner in several ways. The sheer process of discussing ground rules will generate new cultural traits, as doing so creates shared experiences and better understanding of each other. It will also imply that management is using different tools for making the cultural encounter constructive, such as speaking rounds to ensure that everybody contributes, active listening, in-depth questioning and reformulating statements to check understanding. The ground rules sow the seeds of a common language in the new partnership, and will improve everybody's ability to prevent cultural conflicts during the merger process.

The merger between four local authorities in Roskilde, Denmark, provides an example of a merger where new orientation, a clear future perspective and the joint creation of culture played an important role in the merger process. As early as six months before the merger took place, the new top management ensured that a vision and three value statements were formulated for the new joint organisation. They were disseminated to all employees via the common merger news publication, via the chief executive's discussion papers at large management meetings, and via several open after-hours events for employees. The message with the vision and the three value statements was reinforced by strong verbal imagery such as "we're raising the barrier". The heads were gathered several times to discuss the concept of, and to plan for, the cultural integration process, all heads met to start the cultural process together, and expectations of the role of all management at all levels in the culture creation process were set out clearly.

A common concept for cultural seminars for all municipal employees was drawn up with the aim of establishing a shared understanding of the role of culture in the merger as well as shared concepts for what was to take place in all the various workplaces. The seminars were designed to address the aspects of intercultural engagement, cultural understanding and intercultural communication, and some of the concept's fundamental principles were that values and culture must always be seen in relation to work tasks, and that management at all levels was expected to take the lead in the process of change. The cultural seminars were first scheduled for the administrative staff from the various departments, as they would be the first cohort to move together and form new workplaces. The seminars gave management and employees the opportunity to work together on fleshing out the general values by specifying the approaches which the new departments would take to citizens, politicians and colleagues in light of the values. They also fleshed out the values by formulating ground rules for the merger process and the daily collaboration during the early period. Attention was paid to formulating ground rules in both a serious and a humorous manner, and in easily remembered slogans such as "Praise breeds praise".

Managements at all levels have to be extra aware of their role as the bearers of culture. Everything they say and do will be watched keenly, and will influence the creation of the new cultural features, so it is important that they display considerable ability to communicate clearly in an inter-culturally intelligent manner. The first and foremost way in which management can sponsor the creation of a constructive culture is by paying attention to the cultural features of the workplace, and by making culture a legitimate theme to talk about. The concept of managers' sponsorship was introduced in Chapter 3.

An example of clear sponsorship of new values and a new culture was set by a manager who was appointed to a department six months after the merger of two consultancy firms. She found that the newly merged workplace did not live up to the official cultural ground rules on a 'short step from words to action' and 'involvement and joint decision making – the employees are the experts'. She therefore made an attempt to turn the culture in the desired direction by moving her office from the remotest corner with the fine view, into the middle of the corridor close to the coffee machine. She also changed the departmental meetings to include buzz sessions and more listening in her own role. The result was more daily contact between manager and employees and more staff who became involved and raised ideas.

A culture is not created by holding a couple of cultural seminars. The new features must be given time to take root and the process cannot be forced. Time is required as this is not rote learning, but a process of development of intercultural engagement as well as cultural understanding and intercultural communication. It is a search-and-learn process in which the new cultures emerge by experimentation and testing in various contexts, and this is why it is important that the employees should be given scope for working together, crisscrossing the old boundary lines. Conflicts and other critical events must be handled carefully in accordance with the shared ground rules because the new fragile mutual understanding is under special pressure in these situations. Such events are essential in the creation of culture, and the way they are handled will either strengthen the new shared ground rules or weaken them.

Exploring culture in preparation for the merger

Exploring culture is a way in which management and employees can stimulate all three dimensions of their cultural intelligence simultaneously. It is a process in which the parties themselves do the exploration, and thus make a start on the cultural transformation into the new organisation.

The exploration can be aimed at both the parties' own cultures and at the mutual exploration of each other's culture. As mentioned, when a merger is on the horizon, both management and employees become much more aware of the common features of the organisation which they will soon be leaving, and this makes the exploration of their own cultural features relevant. It is a good idea to put our own cultural features into words. It makes them visible and prevents us from defending them by reflex and unconsciously as the only way of doing things. The descriptions should include positive as well as negative aspects of our own culture in order to clarify what we want to bring with us into the new shared culture, and what we will be happy to say goodbye to. It is important not to let the old organisation's culture assume idyllic dimensions on a par with 'the good old days'. The goodbye to the old must be nuanced to prevent it from becoming a heavy drag, impeding the formation of a new sense of community in the new organisation.

It is often a good idea to get help in the exploration of culture from an external process consultant who is not wearing the organisation's cultural 'glasses', and so is able to provide professional guidance for the setting of frameworks and for reflection on the elements which the parties involved find in their exploration.

Whether exploring our own or the other party's cultures, the exploration should start with making the purpose of the process clear in a manner which will both increase the intercultural engagement (curiosity, motivation, and the desire to learn) and the cultural understanding (general knowledge about the role of culture and cultural self-awareness).

Exploring our own culture

Putting our own culture into words can often be difficult at first, and using a model can be a great help in starting. One such is Culture Bridging Fundamentals©, which is discussed later, but other models can also be used. The model should contain some organisational features of particular relevance in connection with the actual merger.

Exploration can take the form of a process stretching over some period in which selected employees interview management and employees around the organisation, after which they gather their impressions together and open joint discussions at seminars. They can also take the form of joint seminars in the form of large group processes, where employees with different job functions interview, reflect and gather impressions in various constellations, out of which an understanding of their organisation's culture will gradually emerge.

If the cultural exploration in one's own organisation is the prelude to a merger, it is important that the summing up is done in a manner which will stimulate the intercultural engagement in relation to the other merger parties, and that the description of the organisation's own cultural features promotes cultural understanding, especially the feel for cultural situations, in order to improve the participants' ability to discover where cultural differences are at play in cross-cultural encounters with the other parties. Knowing one's own culture should preferably lead to better intercultural communication, and therewith to the ability to turn off the autopilot and find more options for action in cultural encounters.

Exploring each other's cultures

Exploring each other's cultures is an obvious starting point on the cultural transformation. In so doing, we learn about each other, prick ballooning preconceptions, and create trust. The process is similar to the rituals of our prehistoric ancestors when the tribes went visiting and revisiting each other, exchanging gifts in preparation for intertribal weddings. In the modern version, the merger process, we also visit and revisit each other, keeping eyes and ears open. We may explore the other organisation's practice in given situations such as meetings and decision-making processes, or ask how they tackle disagreements or show appreciation. The methods can be observation, interviews, or focus group dialogues.

The mutual exploration can be prepared by the parties together so that it follows the same lines, or the parties can each plan their own exploration; but whichever method is used, it is important to ensure that the exploration involves a joint discussion of the features which have been found, and dialogues on what is important for either party in the new organisation.

The journey of exploration into the other culture can take the form of *appreciative interviews*, in which employees tell each other of results of which they are proud. This will not only increase the parties' understanding of each other and each other's former work conditions, but also clarify what 'crown jewels' are worth bringing into the new organisation. Appreciative interviews are good at creating contact without triggering the other person's defences, and many new stories will be discovered to inspire hope of the new and indicate directions to follow.

The aim of the mutual cultural exploration is to improve the intercultural engagement of all participants in that their mental flexibility and interest in understanding each other grows, and cultural understanding will develop in that the participants are confronted with themselves and the others as cultural beings in many ways. The different forms of being together will train different aspects of their intercultural communication, especially their ability to build common ground in cultural encounters.

Analysis of one's own and others' cultural features brings culture into the open professional space and brings relevant aspects to light which might otherwise be left to brood in gossip and other indirect and unfruitful ways. Talking about differences and cultural features and putting the difficulties we meet into words allows them to become more legitimate.

Applying a model for understanding

A model can contribute to cultural understanding by offering a set of categories for developing a deeper cultural self-awareness, and awareness of the other party, and thus also for developing flexibility in understanding by enabling participants to see situations in a broader perspective. Culture Bridging Fundamentals (CBF) is a model developed for clarifying important cultural differences between merging organisations. The model was developed by the international consultancy firm Intercultural Management Associates (ICMA) on the basis of many years of experience in merger processes (Gancel et al., 2002 and www.icmassociates.com).

Culture Bridging Fundamentals© is a support tool for assisting people from different organisational units in gaining better insight into how they are alike, and which of their cultural features are especially different. The categories offer a common language for the cultural integration process, and thereby contribute to the intercultural communication. Insofar as these categories usually make good sense for the people involved, their use will stimulate the intercultural engagement, especially participants' curiosity and motivation for building common ground.

The model points to features which show up between different national cultures as well as between organisational cultures and functional cultures. It is based on the fact that there are three important challenges which have a decisive influence on whether the merging parties will succeed in creating a constructive community and an efficient new organisation. The three challenges are:

- Legitimacy, the aspect of reliability and authority. Whom do we trust? Who should lead? Whom will we follow?
- Effectiveness, the aspect of problem solving and decision making. How do we get things done here? How do we get results?
- The future, the aspect of survival and development. What will make people believe that this organisation has a future? How do we communicate the organisation's goal and how do we get people to back up around it?

Each challenge can be divided into three different preferences – cognitive, relational or pragmatic – resulting in three different ways of dealing with the challenge.

Legitimacy

Intellectual merits

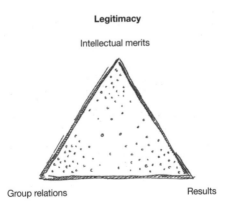

Group relations   Results

Legitimacy. The elements which provide reliability and authority are:

- Group relations: being 'one of our own' via a shared educational background, seniority/experience or social grouping.
- Intellectual merits: having formal academic qualifications, titles and proven expertise, for example in making impressive speeches.
- Results: having shown measurable results or performed significant feats.

Effectiveness

Systems & procedures

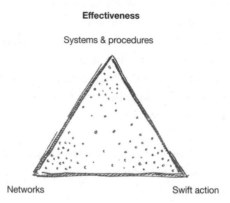

Networks   Swift action

Effectiveness: the way in which problems are solved and decisions made:

- Using networks: networking with people we trust, no matter if we have to criss-cross the formal chains of command.
- Systems and procedures: using the formal chains of command and the fixed procedures.
- Swift action: getting things done, trial or error, or putting out the fire.

Organisational structures

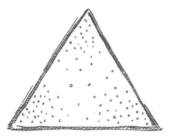

Tradition & identity   Strategic goals

Future: the things which make you believe in the organisation's future:

- Tradition and identity: holding on to one's own heritage, values and principles, doing what normally works well.
- Organisational structures: establishing the right structure and maintaining the organisational charts. Having job descriptions and career programmes.
- Strategic goals: having visions and goals as well as expectations and success criteria clearly formulated and communicated throughout the organisation.

The analysis of an organisation's culture on the basis of this model will show where its preferences within the three challenges are right now, and it may well be a combination of two preferences, for example that a combination of 'networking' and 'swift action' is used in problem solving. There is no link between the preferences. An organisation displaying the cognitive preference in relation to one challenge need not do so in relation to the other two.

> In a merger between banks, a Danish executive from one of the companies was surprised to find that his Finnish middle managers from the other bank had already implemented a decision which they had spoken about, but which was not yet final as far as he was concerned. They said, "But you said you preferred this decision and you're the boss." And he answered, "Yes, I did, but it's your responsibility to give me the necessary information about the conditions in Finland so that we can avoid making the wrong decision. Your professional expertise is necessary."

The situation was due to cultural differences between the two organisations. Whether the differences were largely national or organisational is not important. Where the Finnish middle managers based legitimacy on authority and titles ('intellectual merits'), the Danish executive was more interested in who had the most important knowledge in relation to getting the best results, regardless of who in the hierarchy possessed that knowledge ('results'). Under the 'effectiveness' dimension, it was important for the Danish executive that decisions were taken formally before being implemented ('systems and procedures'), while the Finnish middle managers clearly preferred 'swift action' without bothering about formalities.

These misunderstandings could perhaps have been avoided if a cultural analysis had been made of the two organisations at the start of the practical integration process. It would at any rate have prepared the parties for the fact that they held different views on decision-making processes and executive authority, and made it possible to adjust mutual expectations.

Follow-up on and implementation of cultural traits

As noted above, it takes a long time from the day when the merger is physically in place until the new shared cultural features emerge. In the early stages, both managements and employees have plenty to do keeping production going while adjusting to new colleagues, new surroundings, new procedures and new task allocations. The technical systems may be playing up and, in short, many are under heavy pressure. This can lead to short circuiting in the efforts to work together, as people forget to use their cultural intelligence. Values and ground rules may have been agreed for the new partnerships, but in the heat of the battle, daily operations and the handling of problems take first priority. It is therefore important to focus on how the implementation of the values is proceeding in the new units and on how well the new cultural features are developing, especially throughout the first year or so. It is wise to take the ground rules up for revision and checking if new agreements are needed. The tender constructive cultural features must be strengthened in order to grow and spread, and it may be necessary to remove some shoots. If dissatisfaction and conflicts are once allowed space to grow, it is more difficult to redress than if they are nipped in the bud. Management should take steps to arrange a number of situations for following up on the merger process, for taking the temperature of the new shared culture in this way becomes a regular part of the culture itself.

This can, for example, be done in a seminar where everybody contributes his or her own experiences from the early period in the merged organisation in a manner which will generate greater cultural understanding across the boundary lines. This status process can be started in pairs or small groups, in this way increasing personal contacts across any problems and thus strengthening the intercultural engagement. When the total picture of the state of the new cultural features is put together, it is helpful to introduce new methods for strengthening the intercultural communication in the ordinary working day. It is important that the process is designed such that the seminar itself reflects and strengthens the unit's desired cultural features.

Appreciative interviews will contribute to the development of all three dimensions of cultural intelligence, as they give the participants a rare insight into how a person with a differently composed cultural background thinks and acts. The participants see more sides of each other and get in behind any stereotypical perceptions. They may also gain an opportunity to learn how an event can be given quite a different interpretation to their own.

If the appreciative interview is to be used shortly after the merger, the questions could look like this:

You have probably experienced both good and not-so-good situations, pleasant surprises, stagnation and perhaps even disappointment. Please try now to think of a situation during the merger process so far which was particularly positive for you.

- What was the situation?
- Which persons were involved?
- What did you do? What did the others do?
- What was the result?
- How did you feel while it was happening and just after?
- What made it work so well?
- What sides of yourself did you use?

The interviews should be made in pairs, with one person interviewing the other for about 10–20 minutes, after which they change roles and the other person is interviewed for 10–20 minutes.

In presenting the results of the interviews, the positive things must be expressed in words, and the presentations should be followed by a discussion and agreements on how more of these constructive elements can be created in the new unit.

5/

CROSS-NATIONAL
CULTURAL ENCOUNTERS

Apart from the relationship between the genders, hardly any area is more heavily loaded with stereotypes than the relationship between nationalities or ethnicities

In this chapter, we discuss the question of how to act in a culturally intelligent manner in cross-national cultural encounters within and between organisations. We also discuss how to relate to general patterns in different cultures without being enmeshed in stereotypical interpretations. Examples will focus primarily on collaborative partnerships within a company, but they are also relevant to partnerships between companies from different countries.

The chapter is in three parts. The first part deals with the two main dimensions of cultural differences, namely practice and forms of understanding. The second part reviews the 'cultural maps' put forward by various experts and the last part describes how we can develop and make use of cultural intelligence in cross-national situations.

The aim of working on cultural issues in cross-national organisations is to lay a foundation for the best possible results, either because the organisation has found that cultural differences create difficulties in working relationships, or because it believes that constructive cultural encounters will produce synergy and creativity. It follows that the main goal of such work is to establish a shared framework of understanding in order to facilitate collaboration and productivity.

Apart from the relationship between the genders, hardly any area is more heavily loaded with stereotypes than the relationship between nationalities or ethnicities. "Typically American style that…", "You Europeans always act like…". If an Italian is late for some meetings, it will be interpreted as a national characteristic. If a Finn is late, it will be seen as a personal idiosyncrasy, not as an expression of his culture. These stereotypes or preconceptions have not dropped out of thin air. Every culture consists of a series of norms, social conventions, language and thought patterns which are characteristic of its members, even when they move outside their own cultural circles. But as different cultural features are generalised and turned into stereotypes, they also become value charged. Stereotypes arise as boundary markers in the encounter between different groups: "They're like that and we're like this", and – by implication – "Our way is better than their way in the vast majority of cases". Stereotypes are never neutral, and the weight of values which they bring into a cultural encounter makes it difficult to establish a genuine rapport. "Don't mention the war" is an often-heard British joke, which may make a German smile politely, but which will hardly make him feel included.

Getting behind the stereotypes is a challenge which requires both intercultural engagement and intercultural understanding – two of the dimensions of cultural intelligence. It is not easy. Apart from serving as boundary markers between groups, stereotypes also fulfil a need for mental coordinates in a complex world. By sorting people into 'categories', we create a mental reference map, as the Norwegian Thomas Hylland-Eriksen describes it (2003: 34). The Danish newspaper *Weekendavisen* (WA 52, 2006) published an article about a Danish executive stationed in Georgia. He was working under highly difficult conditions, and the journalist asked him how he managed to stay on and to be successful. His Georgian driver Irakli had the following explanation:

"I suppose it's because Danish people have Viking blood in their veins. It's necessary; the others turned tail and ran… From the West, only the Danes have managed to do business here. You're used to conquering new territory."

The Danish executive also uses a stereotype to explain why he is in Georgia:

> "But you must understand that I've taken no active decision not to want to work in Denmark. It just happened like this. Perhaps because I'm from Jutland. We Jutlanders grab a good offer when we get one."

These examples of stereotypes in daily language show how automatic the descriptive concept of culture is. Culture is seen as a quality with independent explanatory value. The executive acts the way he does because he has Viking blood in his veins (one wonders what his family tree looks like), and because he is from the Jutland. He then adds a regional stereotype on top of the national one for good measure – "People from Jutland are tougher than other Danes" – thus rhetorically confirming his sense of identity.

The closer two cultures are to each other, the greater the risk of misinterpretation. The similarity lulls us into the belief that we're practically alike, so we don't activate our curiosity, but leave the autopilot on. Recently, the media in Southern Sweden have shown an interest in the cultural differences between Denmark and Sweden, and an article in the *Sydsvenskan* announced under the heading "All cultural conflicts finally mapped":

> Danish executives are authoritarian. They rarely listen to their employees and they can fire people without reason. On the other hand, they are good businesspeople, good in argument and good at solving conflicts.
>
> *Sydsvenskan*, 23 August 2006

Offering a stereotype with no explanation, this fanfare is of little help if the aim is to develop cultural intelligence.

A Swedish decision-making process is long and drawn out compared with other Northern European and Anglo-Saxon practices because it involves bringing to light all possible solutions and viewpoints before a decision is made – in unanimity. The implementation proceeds, however, more swiftly than in Denmark, because everybody understands what is involved. A Danish decision-making process is quick and characterised by the fact that it is often the boss who does most of the talking, but the decision is not nearly as final as in a Swedish context. In simplistic terms you could say that every decision is the starting point for a new discussion in Denmark. For example, lessons learned from the early implementation phase can lead to the decision being revised. But a Swede who takes part in a management meeting in a Danish organisation and who does not understand the Danish codes will believe that the decisions have the same final stamp as in Sweden, and that there is no room for objections and reflection. This impression will be reinforced in the situation by the fact that Danish meeting behaviour is more expressive and louder than the Swedish, and that consequently, a Danish boss is more likely to raise his voice when concluding than his Swedish counterpart.

Stereotypes create conflicts and block the opportunity of resolving them. People from different national cultures do not have a common set of standards and a common language for conflict resolution, so cultural intelligence is urgently needed. Conflicts which are not basically cultural very easily become so if the ability to develop a bridge-building, conflict-resolving practice is lacking. To get behind the stereotypes, we need other categories to guide us and to work by. We need categories capable on the one hand of encapsulating concrete forms of expressions, and on the other hand of placing these in an interpretative framework. This is the topic of the next section.

Practice and forms of understanding

Systems, whether organisations, families or cultural frameworks, develop habits and routines which gradually become norms, and they develop a common language, part of which is so much an insider's language that only members can understand it. These forms of language are called codes. When new members enter the system (the culture), they must learn the existing norms and codes in order to be accepted as 'full' members. Some systems require its members to master practically all these norms and codes in order to be accepted. This applies in particular to traditional local societies. Other systems, such as most workplaces, have less strictly defined conditions for membership. Culture is thus on the one hand practice – certain ways of speaking, acting and relating to each other. Practice, on the other hand, is related to patterns of understanding, preferences and thought patterns, some of which are explicit and conscious, while others are subconscious. Practice and patterns of understanding affect each other mutually, but not in a linear manner which would allow a certain practice to be deduced from a certain thought pattern or *vice versa*.

Codes

Codes are found within all cultural systems, but in national cultures they are woven together in complicated systems of meaning, and this makes them difficult to break. When a Briton answers "very interesting" to a proposal, other Britons will know better than to persevere with the idea. The answer is simply a polite rejection, a code developed in a culture where open conflicts are avoided as far as possible. But someone from a more explicit culture, for example from The Netherlands, who is used to things being put much more directly, may return from the meeting and tell his colleagues that the proposal was received with interest – with the result that energy is wasted on continuing to work on it.

Codes are found in both verbal and body language. It is confusing for a Scandinavian when people from the Balkans answer affirmatively by moving their heads from side to side almost in a figure of eight. Scandinavians expect a nod for a non-verbal "Yes".

Codes are condensed meaning. They communicate a certain message in ultra-short form. Codes make it easier and quicker to communicate within the cultural group that shares them. "He's very American" is a code met in many places in Northern Europe. It means something like "He's very loud, draws a lot of attention to himself, believes he understands things even if they're far more complicated than he realises – and we don't really like his style." This is an example of a stereotype used as an ordinary code among people of the same nationality about people of other nationalities. Lifting his brows, a Dane may say to another Dane "Poles are all the same!" and the other Dane will understand him immediately, without necessarily agreeing. If, on the other hand, a Brazilian was witnessing this little exchange, he would have no idea what was meant.

In cultural encounters, it is primarily language codes which hold the greatest interest, but the physical world in which we live also contains many codes. In a company, known worldwide for its production of electronic devices, one of the top executives had her office in the basement some years ago. The furniture was probably about 30 years old, and the entire interior showed signs of use and wear. Visitors were surprised that the production and export of top professional equipment was managed from such humble rooms. What was the message of this code? Economy. The company had originally started in a basement on borrowed money, and the founders' struggle to make ends meet during the early phase had made its 'imprint on the culture'. Money was invested in expensive equipment, but everybody was expected to show thrift and economy in their daily routines.

Codes are thus specific forms of expression, the message of which must be decoded to be read by outsiders. The longer a group has existed, the more codes it will have developed, and the more difficult it is – all else being equal – to become a member of the group. Most codes are so familiar that those who use them are not at all aware that they are codes.

A project group comprising a British, an American, a Japanese and two Swedish members was working on cultural integration in an assembly line factory. All meetings were in English, but logs kept of time spent speaking showed considerable discrepancies over time. The Japanese member had spoken least, then came the two Swedes one after the other. The American and British members had each logged the longest speaking times. Nevertheless, it was practically always the two Swedish members' proposals which were adopted. Scrutiny of the group's meetings revealed that the two Swedes very often exchanged a couple of brief comments during the meeting, after which one of them made a proposal which was then passed. They were not themselves aware of what they were doing, and they denied most emphatically that their aim was to dominate the group's decisions. What happened was that the two Swedes were able in no time – thanks to shared national language codes and despite considerable differences in personality – to mutually adjust their ideas. The others, who shared no common code of this nature, never got as far as formulating their own proposals, but satisfied themselves by proposing changes to those of the Swedes.

This example illustrates a very important point about shared codes.

This is the confidence members of the group have in their ability to 'read' other members, whether or not they agree with them. And this confidence builds security.

> A community can also use the shared codes to exclude others consciously or subconsciously. In a Danish department in a multinational American company, management's official language was English in order to accommodate the American top executive. But Danish was the predominant language in all breaks, including the common lunch, and also when organisational issues were discussed. As a result, the American top manager found it difficult to share in important information about the organisation's daily management, and he began increasingly over the years to close himself up in his office with the information which was available to him, namely reports and statistics.

"We have to have a common language." This is a statement often heard when groups or organisations are brought together, and it expresses precisely the need for shared codes. We simply do not understand each other without them. A shared language has its source in shared practice, so if the creation of a shared language is to succeed, steps must be taken to ensure that all who are to use it share in its construction through concrete collaboration.

It takes time to discover codes. A non-Swedish process consultant explains:

"I had worked with Swedish project groups for several years before realising how they knew they had made a decision. As far as I could see, a long discussion took place which then suddenly stopped without any conclusion being announced. Having watched this happen a number of times, I had to ask what the decision had been and whether everybody was agreed. They looked at me in surprise and said 'Yes, of course'. But they were unable to explain how they knew that they were finished. I realised much later that the code for 'decision reached' in a Swedish consensus culture is the fact that nobody has anything further to say. They turn and twist an issue until everyone is on the same wavelength. When this point is reached, there is no reason to say any more."

This is one of the more subtle codes because it lies in what is not said. It is not surprising, therefore, that the group members themselves were unable to explain it. The process is too obvious for them to notice.

Homogeneity or heterogeneity: to be alike or different?

People's own home culture will subconsciously prepare them differently for the development of cultural intelligence and awareness. People can grow up in a place where everybody has fair skin and speaks the same language, or in a place where many skin colours are seen and many languages are spoken. In the former case, another skin colour will be something we notice as different, while in the latter, the normal thing is felt to be that people with different skin colours live side by side. We subconsciously believe the culture we grew up in to be universal or normal.

A Swedish production manager stationed in a joint venture in China had organised the work in self-governing groups based on his good experience with this system from home. To his considerable frustration, however, he found that he had to personally check the quality of the products over and over again. "They are not working in teams at all like they do in Sweden", he complained in irritation. It didn't help to ask if there were any problems

– there never were. The Chinese workers had learned that you do not bring a boss bad news. They preferred to solve all problems as best they could, but in this case unfortunately with consequent quality defects.

The error which the Swedish manager made was to assume that the Swedish model of teamwork was universal. His handicap may be that he comes from a culturally homogeneous country. The Scandinavian countries are star examples of homogeneous countries, by which is meant that the families of the vast majority of the population have been living in the same area for generations. The experience of diversity is not *per se* a guarantee for the development of cultural intelligence. Many heterogeneous cultures, such as that of the United States, are a patchwork of different subcultures which develop and frame their identities in different ways, often through negative demarcations in relation to others. But the differences function together in public and in the workplace, and it is generally assumed that people hold different convictions and have different ways of living, while in a homogeneous culture it is easy to develop the view that uniformity is a fact of life. When asked what makes them most proud of their country, Americans generally answer "freedom", the freedom to think and do whatever you want to. This idea of freedom is egalitarian, all have the same right to 'seek their own happiness', and as Kurt Lewin has demonstrated, this constitutes a general preconception of the foundation on which American society rests.

An example of how difficult it can be to enter a homogeneous society with a heterogeneous culture in the personal baggage is presented by an American who arrived in Sweden after having lived in Brussels for a number of years. She was shocked at how difficult it was to become accepted as a full member of the management group to which she

> belonged. She had a high-level position in a company which had activities on all continents and had expected to meet an 'international' attitude, but she was confronted with a culture where the unconscious expectation was that "we're all alike", and where the criterion for membership was that she understood the local codes.

The pressure to conform is greater in countries with a homogeneous culture – newcomers are not accepted as full members before they have learned all the codes, as the American woman in the above example experienced.

Differences are expected in heterogeneous cultures, and greater allowance is made for them. A typical comment in a homogeneous country is "It's easy to hear that he's Italian". This comment cements the alien difference. He doesn't speak our language the way we do. In contrast, in a heterogeneous culture such as the American, foreigners are given approval for their efforts to speak a foreign language in a cultural encounter. Homogeneous cultures also use a lot of insider humour, for example in the form of irony. People in heterogeneous cultures are more cautious about this.

Forms of understanding: preferences

While codes may be seen as a way of expressing and practising a culture, they are also linked to cultural meaning, to the forms of understanding which characterise that culture. These will now be examined.

When they begin school, children's cultural schooling is already extensive. They have learned a language and most of the social and behavioural norms of the majority culture in which they are growing up. Minority groups may even have 'double schooling', which means that they have acquired (most of) two cultural systems. The children will also have learned the cultural norms of their gender and social class. This early socialisation is not merely mental. It is stored in the body as emotional experiences, a sense of what is right and wrong, what is best and what not to like. Instances of this orientation are called preferences. Some movements have become routine and are easy to do, and others feel awkward, like learning a new dance. Many preferences are explicitly coded as norms, while others are invisible within the child's own cultural group. The term 'preference' includes both implicit and explicit norms.

On top of this – or intermingled into it – comes the influence of the educational system. The child learns at school how to address a teacher, how to ask questions (for example if is it acceptable to ask critical questions), and what forms of emotional expression are socially legitimate.

Some cultural theories speak of values as a basic element. But most run into problems when trying to account for why people do not act in accordance with their values. To explain this discrepancy, Edgar H. Schein, a well-known American organisation expert, uses the concept of 'espoused values', in extension of the concept previously formulated by the – also American – organisation experts Argyris and Schön. We understand this to mean that the early implanted preferences are prior to values. They are anchored in the body before the child has words to express them. When the child learns language, the current norms are explained in value terms: "It is not nice to…"; "In a democratic society, people…". This is how the child learns an ethical codex or a set of values, but it cannot be taken for granted that words and body reactions agree. This is why we speak here of preferences rather than values in order not to confuse the two. This is also the approach taken by the Dutch sociologist Geert Hofstede when he defines values as "broad tendencies to prefer certain states rather than others" (Hofstede, 1994: 8).

There is also another – and more important – problem in using the term 'values' when speaking of cultural differences. When using the term 'value', the phenomenon is raised beyond discussion in the context of cultural differences. Values belong in the sphere of identity: an individual's values cannot be challenged without challenging the individual himself. If, on the other hand, we speak of preferences, it is possible in pure language terms to allow greater flexibility – and there is a strong need of that in cultural encounters. The fact that an individual prefers something above something else is not the same as not being also able to do that 'something else'. An individual preferring direct eye contact is very well able to turn off his autopilot and lower his eyes when speaking to someone else.

Apart from system and power issues in cultural encounters, two types of difficulties remain in cross-national collaborations. One is about understanding each other's codes. The second is about being unaware of our own filters, the blindness caused by our own preconceptions and preferences. In the section below we present several examples of typical traps of both types. The aim is to use these examples to improve cultural intelligence.

Cultural maps

Working on the basis of general cultural categories is like using a large-scale map. The map is a useful and necessary aid for orientation, but we know that as we travel through the landscape, it will unfold in ways which have nothing to do with the map. The same applies when we prepare for a cultural encounter by reading about the foreign culture. We pick up only a few general bearings, but we cannot know what the attitude of the people we meet is, and how they think and act. Another thing which many map readers have found is that landscapes change. Towns grow, new roads are built, and watercourses are rerouted. The map is outdated. Like landscapes, cultures change in response to people's actions and interactions.

Using a map to find your way when driving is intelligent. Using knowledge about the general features of different cultures for guidance is also intelligent, but only if we are constantly aware that a map is not reality. Problems lie in wait for us if we take maps and models to be the reality.

Before we enter the cultural topography, we will briefly introduce the main studies to which we refer.

Probably the most widely quoted expert on cultural maps is the Dutch sociologist Geert Hofstede, who carried out a study of IBM in the 50 countries where the corporation was then represented in the period 1967 to 1973. Using the same organisation for his study enabled him to eliminate several variables which must otherwise be assumed to make a cross-national comparison difficult. He was also able to compare answers from people of the same age, gender and job functions in different countries. Hofstede has later added more countries to his study.

Hofstede defines culture as "the collective mental programming which sets the members of a group or category apart from those of another." Hofstede's programming metaphor is very much to the point insofar as the control system underlying the programme is subconscious, but it is unfortunate in that it suggests a robotic programming: if an individual is programmed to act in a certain way, he or she can act only as programmed. Although there is a logical difference between genetic and social programming, the result is the same: we *are* our culture. If we are programmed into our culture, we are by definition excluded from being co-creators of it. This book argues, however, that this view is fundamentally flawed when seen in relation to how culture arises and develops. Nevertheless, the categories Hofstede has developed to describe national cultures are valuable and recognisable.

Hofstede takes the view that cultural programming accounts for about 50 per cent of the differences he found. The scale applied is thus a large one – offering about as much detail as we get when gleaning from a world map that Costa Rica is located in Central America, but being unable to learn anything more about the country.

Some of the writers who come closest to the code concept adopted in this book are the American anthropologists Edward T. Hall and Mildred Reed Hall who, in their book *Understanding Cultural Differences*, simply state that "Culture is communication" (1990: 3). We communicate via words, material objects and behaviour which are coded expressions for the internal dynamics as well as the written and unwritten laws of a given culture. Hall and Hall therefore study patterns of communication in relation to the general preferences which they find in various national cultures. This practical approach developed by Hall and Hall is a very useful tool for the study of cultural differences.

The same applies to organisation experts' Fons Trompenaars (Dutch) and Charles Hampden-Turner's (British) *Riding the Waves of Culture*, which is also a very useful introduction to national cultural differences. Trompenaars and Hampden-Turner use largely the same categories as Hofstede and Hall and Hall, so their work will not be discussed in any further detail here. The strength in their approach is their detailed description of how to create space for both parties when a cultural encounter involves opposing preferences.

A final work which deserves mention here is Nancy J. Adler's *Organizational Behaviour*. Adler takes her basis in the different situations in which an organisation must handle cultural diversity –

for example a multicultural team, global negotiations, and expatriations – and she couples codes and cultural maps into her suggestions for how to create cultural synergy. Her book is aimed primarily at the American reader, but it contains many accurate observations and descriptions of situations which are also highly useful for other readers. Adler's approach is very close to our view:

> Although we may think that a major obstacle in conducting business around the world is in understanding foreigners, the greater difficulty involves becoming aware of our own cultural conditioning.
>
> Adler, 1997: 80

We provide below a brief overview of the most widely used categories for mapping cultural differences. There will be some overlap between some of the categories used by the present authors due to the fact that their theoretical bases differ. The important thing is not, however, whether a phenomenon can be sharply defined and placed in only one category. Differences in codes can be related to different preferences depending on the context. The important thing is to be aware of the points where significant differences between the national cultures may be found.

Hall and Hall

Hall and Hall focus mainly on three areas in their cultural mapping: high or low context, the meaning of space, and time orientation.

High/low context

All communication takes its meaning from the context in which it occurs: time, place, prehistory, communication partners. The context is the unwritten or tacit 'text' surrounding the spoken text.

In high-context cultures such as Japan, France and the Arab countries, it is necessary to master many codes in order to be able to communicate effectively. In relation to a meeting or negotiations, this means that the participants will be moving round the subject in circles for a prolonged period before getting to what an Anglo-Saxon or Scandinavian would call the 'point'. The round-about talk is partly about getting enough information to be able to form an independent opinion on the matter, and partly about observing each other and building a relationship of trust which is a necessary precondition for collaborating in a communicative culture. In a low-context culture such as the Northern European or the Anglo-Saxon cultures, the discussion has a single purpose. People talk to each other to gain relevant information on a specific topic, and when that is obtained, the conversation stops. A proposal or idea is typically presented in a monologue without interruption from the others. People go directly to the point and do not spend time on small talk (the expression itself reveals the dislike).

> The Spaniard (relatively high context) said at the end of a meeting in a cross-national project group "It was a good meeting – we got to know each other better." The German participant (relatively low context) was also satisfied, but for another reason: "It was a good meeting – we got as far as we'd hoped."

There are numerous stories of the tests of patience to which expatriate Scandinavians have felt exposed when having to work with Middle Eastern or even Southern European colleagues and trading partners. It might help if they were to redefine their concept of what the 'point' is – and book an airline ticket with an open departure date.

The meaning of space

Space is partly about personal space in the sense of how much space we need around us to feel comfortable – how close others with whom physical contact is acceptable may come to us – and partly about the demarcation of territory and positions of power. The location of the chief executive's office is, for example, different in Germany and France. In Germany it is on the top floor to symbolise power. In France it is typically in the centre of the building so that the head is placed at the centre of the communication network.

Respect for personal space is essential for successful human contact. Northern cultures, including Japan, prefer physical distance, while southern cultures prefer being physically close.

Time orientation

Not everybody puts their faith in clocks. In many cultures time is an almost irrelevant category – but events and relations are not. If a man from a polychronic culture meets a friend on his way to work, they will finish their talk before moving on. If the friend needs help with anything, the man will help him and then go on to work afterwards. Hall and Hall call this sense of time, which is oriented towards the things which are happening at the moment and is measured against them, 'polychronic time orientation'. Polychronic time orientation is related to cyclic time, which follows the rhythm of nature in twenty-four hour and annual cycles. The polychronic time orientation is found in all societies where nature is a critical factor, but not only there. The opposite of polychronic time orientation is the monochronic orientation, which follows the clock. Cultures with monochronic preferences prefer to do one thing at a time, whereas polychronic-oriented people are 'multitasking', doing many things in parallel at the same time and preferably together with many people.

A monochronic culture stresses precision and observance of deadlines, and relationships are of only secondary importance in the work context. In a polychronic culture, deadlines are desirable but not absolute.

These differences in orientation to time can give rise to many conflicts – as well as to many stereotypes. The borderline between the monochronic and polychronic orientation in Europe is by and large identical with the boundary line between Protestantism and Catholicism, and as demonstrated by Max Weber in the early 1900s, there is a connection between the Protestant work ethic and the demands of capitalism with respect to punctuality and method of production.

If we fail to understand the difference between the two orientations, we will, as Northern Europeans, easily be piqued at others' arriving too late at a meeting, talking on the telephone during the meeting, or reading papers which have no relevance to the meeting. This behaviour will be an expression of lack of interest or direct disrespect in Northern Europe. Southern Europeans, on the other hand, will find it very boring to attend a meeting with the monochronic Northern Europeans.

During a telephone conference, the Spanish team member apologises for not having delivered on time as agreed. He explains in detail what prevented him – and he clearly expects to be forgiven.

Hofstede

Hofstede calls his five categories 'dimensions of national culture':

- Power distance/social inequality
- Individualism/collectivism
- Masculinity/femininity

- Uncertainty avoidance
- Confucian dynamics

Power distance/social inequality

This dimension measures the degree to which members of a society expect and accept that power is unequally distributed. 'Members of a society' here means the vast majority who do not have any personal power. The dimension is also often described as the difference between hierarchical and equality-seeking cultures.

This dimension is highly relevant to the study of organisations as it directly addresses the issue of power and management. High power distance is, for example, characterised by many hierarchical levels and a generally authoritarian management style, while the utilisation of independent teams and the inclusion of subordinates in the decision-making processes are signs of low power distance.

Power distance is signposted via innumerable codes: who opens a meeting, who speaks most, who asks the questions – and what types of question are asked, when does a superior step into the negotiations, who gives feedback to whom – and at the physical level, how the boss's office is fitted out in comparison with others.

A German engineer was sent out to assist a Japanese customer with the installation of a production plant. He was working with engineers on his own level, and after a couple of days he had formed the certain impression that they had all agreed a solution. But next day, the Japanese engineers had objections to the agreement from the previous day. Gradually the German engineer understood that his Japanese counterparts did not have the power to make decisions, but had to have their superior's acceptance of the solution. They had not, however, advised him of this (Japan is a high context country, where people are expected to be aware of this rule).

When he asked to meet the superior directly, his request was politely but firmly rejected. The problem persisted over several months, and was not solved until the German engineer's superior went to Japan to meet the Japanese superior. Then hierarchy and status matched.

The Protestant countries are coloured by a long history of equality thinking, and for this reason occupy – together with Israel – a relatively low position with respect to power distance when seen in a global context. The belief in authorities is not very strong. What counts is individual performance and qualifications.

Individualism/collectivism

Individualism is used as a description of societies where the bonds between individuals are loose, where it is expected that all people take care only of themselves and their immediate families. In a collectivist society, however, people are integrated from birth into strong, cohesive groups which are expected to protect them throughout life in return for their unquestioning loyalty.

This dimension has an important bearing on the type of reward system we prefer: individual performance-based pay or a more collective group-/organisation-based pay system. Individualism is clearly associated with the old capitalist countries, and considerable differences in orientation will therefore be found, for example in relation to loyalty bonds, between the Western world and all areas where industrialisation has come later (the Middle and Far East, Latin America and Africa). In collectivist societies, family relations and obligations weigh more heavily than the opportunity of winning individual merit.

At the start of a project with participants from Europe, the United States and Japan, the process consultant asked the group members to explain how they understood the task, and what they would gain personally from working on it. The Japanese participant found it difficult to get any meaning out of the second question and answered by giving a lengthy account of what the project would mean for the company and for his superior. The process consultant was puzzled until she became aware that she had just met the difference between an individualistic and a collectivistic preference.

Masculinity/femininity

This dimension is about gender and gender roles as a cultural dimension. Masculine cultures are characterised by self-assertion and competitiveness, while feminine cultures are characterised by modest demands and a caring attitude. Hofstede has been criticised for using these terms, and other writers, including Nancy Adler, prefer to talk of differences between focusing on career and focusing on quality of life.

A British-Norwegian team were close to their deadline. After many unanswered telephone calls to Oslo one Friday afternoon, the British project manager exclaimed "What on earth are they doing after 4 p.m.?!" Not to give priority to work above leisure hours was almost unthinkable for the Briton, while his Norwegian team partner was just as clear in his mind that he should of course be with his family on the weekend. What the Briton did not see was the fact that the Norwegian member started work again when the children had been put to bed.

When the Scandinavian management style is mentioned, it is the feminine dimension which is its particular characteristic (together with low power distance), and this dimension represents its primary difference from the Anglo-Saxon cultures. It is seen in the employee rights legislation, holidays and maternity leave, and it is seen in the weighing of family against career, where the family is given a relatively much higher priority in Scandinavia than in the United States.

There are, however, considerable differences in the weighing of this dimension within Scandinavia and the Nordic countries themselves. Sweden is more feminine in culture than Norway, Denmark or Finland. The difference between Denmark and Sweden, which southern Swedes see as hierarchical – "Danish bosses are authoritarian" – is rather a difference within the masculine–feminine dimension, with Denmark being relatively more masculine.

Uncertainty avoidance

Uncertainty about the future is a general condition of life, but different societies look at it differently. Countries which rate high on the uncertainty avoidance dimension seek to limit uncertainty and ambiguity by having many rules and procedures, or by seeking technological control of their surroundings. In some other countries, people do not feel threatened by uncertainty, and do not seek to gain control to the same extent. Latin America and countries like Belgium, France and Germany score high on uncertainty avoidance, while Great Britain, Sweden and especially Denmark score low on this scale. Hofstede notes that this dimension is irrelevant in countries like China, Japan and Korea, which lie outside the domain of monotheistic religions, and he refers to the latter religions' search for the one truth as an explanation of why they seek to reduce uncertainty.

Organisations can be highly driven by rules and procedures, or they can have a more flexible attitude to the degree of structuring. Different attitudes to, for example, documentation and reporting can thus be the cause of considerable frustration in connection with cross-national collaboration.

> A Danish manager was working with his German counterpart in a company making wind turbine components. He had been told that people in Germany place considerable weight on educational qualifications, so he remembered to list his academic degrees in his email signature to his German colleague in order to give an impression of reliability. This, however, did not satisfy the German. Several emails came back from him asking for further documentation for the plans, and this irritated the Dane because he had to spend more time on it than he was used to in a Danish context.

Confucian dynamics

Hofstede added this dimension after his big IBM study, as he realised that his study had been based on the Western way of thinking which, for example, does not understand basic preferences in Chinese culture. He named the dimension after the famous Chinese teacher Confucius (c.500 BC), and it contains a number of 'virtues' which traditionally distinguish Chinese culture in particular, but also that of neighbouring countries such as Korea and Japan. These virtues include respect for the hierarchy, frugality, perseverance, and a sense of shame, while the position of the individual is considered less important.

> A Northern European on a business trip in China was amazed and impressed after a meeting with a group of Chinese economics students, who lived in the dormitory on campus with no possibility of private space, but they all expressed a high level of gratitude at being able to study so that they would have an opportunity to secure their family's financial

> circumstances and status. The great majority of them had one or more jobs on top of their full-time studies.

It is difficult for a Westerner to comprehend the Oriental mentality, of which 'Confucian dynamics' is an expression. When Western companies attempt to introduce Japanese production systems, they often fail because managers and employees lack the same basic attitude to placing common and long-term goals above individual and short-term ones. Toyota describes "The Toyota Way" thus:

> Success in the Toyota Way has deep roots and derives from a philosophy based on insights into people and their motivation. The Toyota Way is a culture based on long-term philosophy, even if this is at the cost of short-term financial goals.

Today Tomorrow Toyota

Other categories
Diffuse or specific relations: a question of accessibility

The relationship between homogeneous/heterogeneous and the associated preferences is a concept which was dubbed 'diffuse and specific cultures' by Trompenaars and Hampden-Turner (1997: 99 ff.). It is built upon observations made by the social psychologist Kurt Lewin who, following his emigration from Germany to the USA in the early 1930s, made a number of thoughtful observations on the differences between the (middle class) cultures in the two countries.

The distinction concerns what are considered to be public and private zones. In diffuse cultures, to which most European countries belong (Holland being a partial exception), the public zone is relatively small. What people display in public is limited. (Reality TV is a new phenomenon at odds with this preference – and which may have become so popular precisely because it is experienced as barrier-breaking TV.) If a foreigner is invited home by a Scandinavian, she is invited across a threshold behind which, so to speak, she has access to her host's entire life. The visitor can meet her host's friends from other contexts, and when the visitor is met by her host the next day at work, the mutual relationship is more friendly and 'diffuse', that is to say, without sharp borders between the different spheres of life. This is not the case with the Americans, as the following example illustrates.

> On a business trip to the USA, a Scandinavian manager meets a smiling and jovial American in a bright red sweater who presents himself as 'Bob' at an informal 'social dinner'. They talk comfortably together about many things, and the Scandinavian quickly gains the feeling that they have established quite a close relationship. Next day they meet at work, and Bob now behaves entirely differently. He is still obliging, but he is now in a suit, he asks questions and gives orders, he is straightforward and direct, and he looks at his watch a lot. When the Scandinavian makes a cheerful comment about something they talked about the previous day, the only reply he receives is a casual smile.

In a specific culture, specific norms apply to different areas: work is one area, leisure another. Europeans often misinterpret American openness, thinking that the friendliness they meet is general (diffuse). Danes and Norwegians, who like a pleasant chat in the bar and who also prefer to behave informally at work, can have an expectation that the informal relationship will continue when they move on to business, as shown by the above example. They interpret the American forms of expression on the basis of their own set of codes. They also think, for example, that the phrase 'no problem' means the same for them as for an American. In a Danish/Norwegian code, it means "It's within the normal problem area – we'll do it", while in American code it can mean both "I won't tell you how difficult this will be for us", and "I can't see any problems in it right now (but I'm not promising anything)".

Norwegians, Danes, Dutch and Americans are usually direct and explicit in their working relationships and negotiating styles. They go straight into the matter without a lot of beating about the bush. But Americans are far more reticent about expressing feelings, especially dissatisfaction. The inattentive partner can therefore overlook signs of the beginning of distancing, and only later realise that something has gone wrong.

> Two project groups in a global organisation were to present their work to the Swedish general manager. There was a notable difference in how the Swede and the American did so. The American gave a well-structured PowerPoint presentation and reviewed the individual points briefly and systematically. When he had finished, he asked if there were any questions. There were one or two, which he answered briefly and objectively. The Swede commenced his presentation with a little anecdote from the organisation's everyday life and invited an informal dialogue on it. There followed many contributions from the hall, and the conversation moved off at a number of tangents, as a result of which the time allowed for the presentation was exceeded. The Swede behaved diffusely in this context, using forms of address and codes in the same style as he would have used in a talk in a coffee break. The American, on the other hand, used the style of communication which in his eyes was appropriate to the specific event, namely a project presentation for a manager.

The above is a mini-example of the differences in codes which can be associated with the difference between diffuse and specific cultures. No communication problem was involved – both projects were well received – but the difference in style between the American and the Swede indicates that different behaviour is necessary to gain trust in a Swedish and an American company. If the general manager had been American, he would probably not have been satisfied with the Swede's going over the time limit or his more diffuse presentation.

Neutral/emotional cultures

The point here is how much you show your emotions in professional contexts, and how much you distinguish between showing emotions at work and in other contexts. An emotional outburst in professional contexts is not welcome in the Anglo-Saxon countries or the Far East – which can make these cultures difficult to decipher for Dutch and Germans, for example, who are far more expressive.

> At a meeting in a European mixed-nationality management group, the German member asked the other group members for a clear indication of their opinion on the company's new basic values. The British group members expressed themselves in terms such as "an excellent initiative", "absolutely desirable", "perhaps we might also consider…", and the German manager, who had expected a much more concrete indication, began to argue strongly and loudly for his wish. Tensions rose noticeably in step with his voice, and after a brief period, the highest ranking of the British members suggested a break. Talk during the break revealed that the British members had felt uncomfortable not because of the issue as such, but because of the manner in which it had been put.

Neutral cultures prefer not to show emotions in public. This is seen in many ways. British humour typically relies on 'understatement' with an inbuilt ironic distance, while the Italians prefer to be expressive about their emotions. The same difference in preferences is evident in dialogues. Nancy Adler notes the following observations from a study by John Graham (Adler, 1997: 218):

The speaking partners take turns talking. This pattern is found for example in the United States and Sweden.

The speaking partners take turns talking, with a break between each speaker. This pattern is found particularly in the Far East.

The speaking partners overlap each other. The pattern is typically found in Southern Europe, Latin America – and Denmark.

Performance/ascription

Apart from the categories already noted, Trompenaars and Hampden-Turner include the concepts performance/ascription. This category deals with how to achieve status in the eyes of the community. Performance-oriented status is based on what an individual has achieved, his CV and his track record. Ascribed status is achieved by virtue of membership of, for example, a class or a family, or by having studied at a particular university. The Indian caste system is an extreme example of ascription which has nothing to do with the individual's own qualities or efforts.

Scandinavians are not used to behaving in accordance with hierarchical differences deriving from relationships outside work (including age), and they therefore easily come to appear disrespectful in their behaviour in ascriptive cultures.

> Two Japanese were placed in the same group in an international management course. The younger hardly spoke in the other's presence, and never before the older one had spoken. A gentle explanation of the rules of the game in the context in question was required before this pattern changed.

Cultural intelligence in cross-national partnerships

The incentive for ensuring constructive cultural encounters in cross-national organisations is clear: without them, the required synergy and productivity are not achieved. Nancy Adler (1997: 105) describes three basic attitudes in the handling of cultural diversity:

- The provincial: "Our way is the only way."
- The ethnocentric: "Our way is the best way."
- The synergistic: "Creative combinations of our way and their way can be the best way to go."

Adler defines the last way as follows: "Culturally synergistic solutions should be novel and transcend the behavioural patterns of each of the root cultures" (1997: 112), a statement which is fully in line with our concept of cultural intelligence. This section will describe a number of practical approaches which promote co-creation and synergy.

> Two IT departments in a Danish–German organisation joined together to clear up the mutual friction which was disturbing their partnership. They were at pains to avoid stereotypes by investigating the situations where the conflicts were arising, and asking specifically about each other's

interpretations of them. Following a successful meeting, one of the Danish participants said "It was as if we weren't using the codes we usually speak in because others were present. We have to be careful about making smug comments. It was very uplifting to discover that we actually had a common goal."

This is an example of culturally intelligent communication, containing as it did both motivation and engagement – namely the desire to create a better partnership, awareness of their own patterns which can inhibit understanding, and a practice where the group switched off the autopilot and asked active questions instead of acting on their preconceptions.

In cross-national contexts, everything takes longer than in a monocultural context. There are frequent language difficulties, and there are always several codes to be cracked to achieve mutual understanding. Even such elementary concepts as 'meeting' and 'decision' have different meanings in different countries.

A Danish process consultant was in the process of formulating the relational and practical ground rules in a group with very mixed nationalities when he was asked this question by an Italian: "How should 'rules' be understood?" The consultant was astonished, but then realised his own unconscious preconception: when people in a negotiation situation reach agreement on key principles, everybody will try to comply with the principles. No sanctioning authority is necessary. This preconception derives from a Danish cultural context which is distinguished by a sense of equality and individual responsibility. The Italian asked the question on the basis of a far more hierarchical culture, where rules are typically associated with sanctions.

Development of culturally intelligent practice

A range of different tools and methods can be used to develop cultural intelligence in a cross-national management or project group which must be able to work together as a team. Below we describe some of these and explain how they combine the various dimensions of cultural intelligence. The primary focus is on how to integrate the cultural dimension into a partnership so as to achieve results, but we will also touch on how to prepare managers and employees more generally for cross-national collaboration via planned activities within a course framework. The approaches and methods considered below are:

- Opening the cultural field
- Exploring important codes
- Ground rules
- Time for reflection and evaluation
- Support from a process consultant
- Cultural understanding in a course context
- Building relationships
- Feedback

Opening the cultural field

First of all the cultural field must be opened to dialogue and exploration. It can be tempting to jump directly into the work on the assumption that "we have a common goal, and it will overshadow any cultural differences". The fear of magnifying any differences by talking about them may also contribute to this temptation. But whatever the reason for failing to include cultural questions on the agenda, they will nevertheless appear, perhaps in ways the parties would rather have avoided.

Being aware of differences is the best approach to getting the best out of them. If we are not aware, we misunderstand each other, lose tempo and time, and miss the opportunity for learning and benefiting from unexpected viewpoints and ideas. Nancy Adler writes that "In approaching cross-cultural situations, effective businesspeople therefore *assume differences until similarity is proven*." (1997:71). But people who are different may well have interests in common, which of course is the very basis of cross-national collaboration. But unless the partners find a common language in which to communicate, the shared interests will come to nothing/never materialise.

In other words, it is necessary to talk about the fact that different cultural codes and preferences will be at play, and that it is important to listen for these in order to avoid misunderstandings and to gain optimal benefit from the collaboration. It will also be important to specify that the aim is not for everybody to adapt themselves to fit into one dominant culture, but to create a field of work where everybody will be able to contribute – a common ground. The first important ground rule for intercultural communication is for the group to agree that it is OK to put the working process on hold and ask questions if something is not understood. This applies both to language (the group's working language will not be everybody's mother tongue) and to situations where a member becomes confused or uncertain that a particular code may have escaped him.

Exploring important codes

Some central processes must be dealt with in any result-oriented collaboration in a company. The fact that they are central implies that every culture has developed codes for handling them, but the codes differ from company to company and from culture to culture. So it is important to be aware of what means what and how to proceed in any given situation. This is about the engagement and awareness dimensions of cultural intelligence.

Important code systems in organisational relations are:

- How are decisions made – how does the process look?
- How are proposals put forward?
- How is disagreement or criticism expressed?
- How is appreciation shown?
- How are conflicts handled?

A simple way to clarify these questions is to ask the group members from the different national cultures to answer the questions on how they tackle these processes on their professional home grounds. Some differences will emerge immediately. The example below was produced at an international management seminar. It shows differences in relation to decision making and proposals and is by no means representative:

Britons: We present our contributions one by one, often in the form of a PowerPoint presentation. We discuss, but it's the boss who makes the final decision. Decisions must be written down. Proposals can be put forward and changed during the meeting.

Germans: Structured documentation is placed on the table, and reasoned proposals must be submitted in writing in advance to allow people time to prepare. Each member is held responsible. We aim for consensus, but it sometimes happens that we take a vote on an issue.

Italians: We hold big animated discussions. The meaning lies in the body language, not so much in the words said. We make quick intuitive decisions – which may then be changed later. If we make a proposal, we'll generally have discussed it with the boss and others before the meeting.

French:The boss makes the decision by gathering information from different people before meetings.The meeting itself is merely a ritual confirmation of the decision. So it's safe to discuss it loudly – it changes nothing. The boss doesn't like being surprised by new proposals at the meeting.

Danes:We make quick decisions and they are not necessarily put on paper.The discussion often continues after the decision is made, and may lead to it being changed later. Most proposals surface during the discussion and the meetings are rarely very well prepared.

It is clear from this that perceptions of what a meeting really is differ widely.Whether, as in France, the meeting is largely a ritual dance where the work is done in advance outside the meeting room, or as in Germany and Denmark, where it is an important forum for discussing and testing the basis for the decision. It is thought-provoking that such a fundamental and widespread organisational tool is so far from being something about which we can take for granted that we know the rules. How then will it be with elements such as strategy, team, management, project, follow-up, feedback and many others? This is where we need a common language.

When exploring the different codes and preferences, we are, as previously mentioned, working on the engagement and understanding dimensions of cultural intelligence. Having done this, we have a more informed basis on how to work together in the group in question. But it is necessary to look more closely at the intercultural communication in the group, and this is done by formulating a set of ground rules.

Ground rules

The players in a group have different ideas of their roles and responsibilities, and the members will each bring with them their present preconception of their own identity and how things should be done. A forum must therefore be established for negotiating a set of common rules which must be visible to all. We can also call this forum a meta-level, a plateau raised above the level of work, where the group can talk about how they talk. If this plateau is not established, the culture which is strongest in the situation (typically that of the boss) will win.

Management and other key people in organisations are generally not used to setting ground rules as frameworks for working together. To move on to a meta-level is felt as a disruption in relation to the group task which is of course what brings the people together. Time for reflection will never quite fit into the working rhythm. It is therefore necessary to insist on this process. It will take time at the start, but in the long run much time will be saved which would otherwise be spent on adjusting the course, clarifying misunderstandings and resolving conflicts. So if the group is to work together for a prolonged period it is an important investment.

The ground rules must cover the central processes discussed above:

- Decision making
- Presentation of proposals
- Expressing disagreement

- Handling conflicts
- Expressing appreciation.

Furthermore, it is necessary to agree on how to change the ground rules. It may also be relevant for the group to agree on certain areas which individual team members see as important factors for their engagement and ability to contribute with their competences. These can include:

- Degree of punctuality
- Telephone conversations during meetings
- Form and content of feedback.

Quite apart from the fact that a negotiable set of ground rules improves the quality of meetings, the discussion about the ground rules itself promotes greater intercultural understanding as well as greater mutual engagement, in that it is necessary for all to involve themselves in the discussion, and because the discussion invites everybody at the meeting to address issues which are otherwise mostly dealt with around the coffee machine.

Time for reflection and evaluation

Differences will of course continue to pop up in the group's daily work, so it is also important to make a rule which sets time aside regularly for reflection and evaluation of group communication.

This can be done by inserting some time-outs in the group's work to allow the members to reflect on their own work process, if there are things they do not understand, or things they would prefer to do in a different way.

We recommend never closing a meeting in a cross-national group without setting time aside for this kind of evaluation and reflection. What this means is that it must be a natural part of the group's fixed agenda on a par with business-related items. This is unlikely to be something members of the group are used to, but it is the best way to keep focus on the fact that a mutual learning process is also taking place; and the time invested in preventing misunderstandings is saved from time spent on resolving them.

Support from a process consultant

A better result will generally be achieved if a process consultant or facilitator is attached to the group to steer vital phases of the process and assist group members in becoming aware of codes and differences in codes. It is difficult to keep attention on codes when concentrating on the content, and training is required for 'catching a code in flight'. The best 'Aha' experiences in relation to codes occur when we stop the moment they appear, and then examine what they mean.

It is a definite advantage to have someone who is neutral in relation to the various functions, positions and cultural backgrounds in the group. This is where the consultant can assist in preventing group members who dominate in terms of language from also dominating the work. Cross-national groups usually use English as their working language, and there are enormous possibilities for misunderstandings because the subtle aspects of language are overlooked. For that reason, the group is working on a more basic level and need to check definitions and the meaning of important words.

A cross-national management group in a global technical company discussed the establishment of a database in which they wanted to store all the firm's experience with various machinery and production lines for use in different countries. With the Britons and their dominant language competence in the lead, the group soon started structuring the database, ignoring a comment by a Frenchman who was saying in very poor English that the problem was not technical but communication related. The group was stopped by the process consultant and asked to take more time to listen to the less fluent members, and the French member's point ended by becoming the guiding light for the further work.

It is difficult for people whose mother tongue is the organisation's working language to understand and remember what it means for their colleagues that they are unable to express themselves freely and without effort. Many are embarrassed at their lack of fluency in, for example, English, and they shy away from more complicated arguments. It takes discipline on the part of everybody to maintain a slower tempo than would be kept in a monolingual group, and to make regular stops to check how well they understand each other.

Cultural intelligence in a course context

If more time is available, as is the case with courses and management development programs, it is possible to arrange various types of cultural 'voyages of discovery'. Some examples of these are given below.

As a general principle, the best way to learn is to work with things yourself. We are inspired by the Action–Reflection–Learning™ system (ARL) developed by the MiL Institute. The system understands learning as a search process moving back and forth between concrete experiences and abstract conceptualising. Reflection is the process of connecting the two. When using ARL principles, we ask people to make meaning of the questions arising from their own practice and experience. Theoretical concepts (like the definition of culture) are offered to support this process – but not before people have reflected on their own experience, and not as 'truths'. When it comes to developing cultural intelligence, it is especially important to put people in situations where they actually experience that culture is something created in cooperation, and that the best results are obtained via a committed, inquisitive collaboration under manual control. It is necessary, in other words, to talk about cultural intelligence before talking about the cultural map.

Cultural voyages of discovery

The biggest hurdle in developing cultural intelligence is, as noted, recognising one's own cultural ballast and subconscious preconceptions. This only happens when meeting something different. This type of meeting can be planned – for example, as a 'cultural expedition'. When a cross-national team meets in one of the respective countries, the team members are asked to go out in pairs and interview random people on the street about how they see their national culture. After returning home, they tell each other about their observations and discuss what is similar and what is different relative to their own country. This exercise has been successfully used in many different countries, and has awoken the participating managers' surprise, curiosity and desire to explore. An important point is that the exercise gives them the opportunity to be 'research pioneers' outside the context of work, in a field where they have no prestige, competitiveness or anything else at stake. This gives them a greater opportunity to put themselves in an open and listening mindset and let go of their autopilot. The sample questions given to help them start have included:

- What makes you proud to be an American/Belgian/… ?
- How do you see your country as different from others?
- How is success achieved in this country?

This exercise can also be performed with 'native' participants. They have sometimes elected to speak English rather than use their own language. When the exercise is debriefed, some patterns often start to appear, giving cause for reflection on both one's own and the foreign culture.

Another exercise consists of answering two questions within each culture and then exchanging answers. The questions are:

- What do we think you think about us?
- What do we think is important that you should know about us – which we don't believe you know?

Other awareness-generating exercises are mutual interviews which, for example, can concern preferences with respect to managerial behaviour ("What makes a good manager at your place, and what doesn't he/she do?"), handling conflicts ("How are conflicts perceived at your place, and what's done when they occur?") or problem solving ("What has to be present before you call something a problem, and what do you do about it?").

Cultural maps

The introduction of cultural maps functions best when those present have some concrete experiences on which to build – either, and preferably, from direct collaboration with people from other cultures or in the form of an exercise. A comment must be made about the use of Hofstede's categories. They are difficult to use directly in a training situation (which Hofstede himself also warns against) because they easily come to appear as a kind of answer list which calls up stereotypes. Hofstede's material is therefore most suitable as educational material going into greater depth after working more practically with codes and cultural differences which have been experienced.

Cultural games

Different types of games can be used to create awareness of cultural differences. These games are typically constructed such that the participants are divided into groups, where they first agree on some features which are characteristic of their 'culture' (ways of greeting, ways of saying 'no', an important hero myth), and then testing different meetings with the other groups' 'cultures'. The idea of using games is to find a neutral ground to work on by not referring to any of the cultures represented in the room, hence not stepping on anybody's toes through stereotyping. This approach can be very good in connection with an introduction, but when going into a real-life collaboration project it is necessary to have a grip on the codes and preferences that are present among the people in the group.

Building relationships

There is a substantial difference in how a professional relationship is perceived in different countries. As soon as you move out of the northern European and Anglo-Saxon world, where 'the matter' carries more weight than the relationships, you meet people who consider a good personal relationship a prerequisite for a good working relationship. There is therefore good reason to consider how to organise meetings and seminars so that they also consider the social dimension, not merely as a 'happy hour in the bar', but as an integral part of the actual work process.

If you are lucky enough to have the time frame that a managerial development programme provides, it is possible to work quite intensively on relationship building. When this takes place within the same company, the result is a qualitative network building which has an enduring effect in the working relationships. It should be noted that this also applies in 'cold' matter-oriented cultures!

One way of doing this is to work with life stories. In a nationally mixed group of manageable size (6–7 people), the participants are asked to tell one another about their backgrounds and important events in their lives. They are given some questions to prepare themselves, and the rule must be set that no-one has to reveal more than she herself is prepared to reveal. Example questions are:

- What significance did work have in the home where you grew up?
- What expectations did/does your family have for you?
- What people did you meet who were particularly significant for the way you see yourself as a manager?

Sharing such stories means that the participants gain knowledge of each other as individuals, and can mirror themselves in each other's stories. It will create a bonding beyond national and other cultural differences, and this approach makes it difficult to stereotype each other later.

A Brazilian says to a colleague in a concluding feedback round: "It was your personal story which caught my attention – what you said about your son and how much you love him."

A Japanese manager writes about his experience in a managerial development programme that started with life stories: "It was the first time that I was with a group of people of so many different backgrounds – culture, function, careers. It was exciting for me to encounter other ways of thinking. On one level there are big differences between Asia and Europe, East and West – on another there are differences between individuals, and when you get to know the individuals you learn that the 'big' cultural differences are not so important. I know now that I can trust people on the other side of the world." (Rohlin et al., 2002: 128)

The keyword is trust, and trust is created in the same process where shared codes are developed. The investment is engagement and curiosity, and the gain is rapport building and understanding of each other – which make it possible to generate results together over long distances, where the most frequent communication tool is the sterile email.

Feedback

Being able to give each other feedback on communication and behaviour is considered in a Scandinavian context to be an important management and collaboration tool. This also applies in cross-national contexts, but there are very substantial differences in how feedback is perceived in different countries. In the USA, for example, feedback on work performance is quite direct – but very reticent when it comes to something seen as personal. When Americans talk about feedback, they therefore mean speaking about the work which was performed in relation to the goals which were set, not getting to know how other people perceive and react to the mode of communication. In China, feedback on work performance will immediately be seen as something applying to the whole individual.

Feedback can be a big help when it comes to developing relationships and cultural understanding; but in order to succeed, it is first necessary to decode the concept on the basis of the different approaches among those involved, and from there to achieve clarity about what the different people will consider to be constructive feedback. In this area special ground rules must actually be established to make it work constructively.

'Feedback' was included in the programme at an internal company management course with many different nationalities. The instructors placed emphasis on the formulation of feedback in 'I' terms and acting on what an individual does, not on how she is (for example: "I feel encouraged when you support me in persisting in my proposal"). They had also prescribed a strict and simple way of formulating the feedback: "I would like you to continue by doing… because it gives me…" and "I would like you to do more/less of… because it will give me…". Notwithstanding this – by Scandinavian standards – gentle and respectful approach, the Anglo-Saxon members of the group were very nervous, and one of them later said "Ow! I survived – it was actually quite fun once I tuned into it."

It is never possible to cover yourself 100 per cent against misunderstandings and actions that will be perceived by others as crossing the line. It is not possible to acquire cultural intelligence merely by study. We therefore conclude this section by repeating that in cross-cultural contexts, it should always be agreed from the start that it is permissible to ask questions when expressions, codes and patterns of behaviour are not understood.

6/

DEVELOPMENT OF CULTURAL INTELLIGENCE

The optimal approach is to develop cultural intelligence
through a joint effort

The three theme chapters all present different models and tools for the development of culturally intelligent practice within the relevant field. This chapter provides some general considerations on the development of cultural intelligence and on how the various approaches can be used in other areas. It also offers some reflections on how individuals can develop their cultural intelligence as well as how the development of cultural intelligence can be tackled on an organisational basis.

In practice, the three dimensions of cultural intelligence are interwoven, and *intercultural engagement*, *cultural understanding* and *intercultural communication* all interact when cultures meet. This was illustrated in Chapter 1 by a circle with no starting point in order to stress the point that the dimensions should be seen as an interlocking system where all the dimensions are continuously affecting one another. In a cultural encounter, this means that there are three different entry points for improving contact and cultural bridge building.

The development of cultural intelligence can be stimulated in many different ways, and it can originate in experiences in any of the three dimensions. Lack of knowledge of different cultures or a 'bad experience' can make us feel more insecure and make us want to try to avoid intercultural contacts of the same type as those which were unsuccessful, but an unsuccessful intercultural meeting can, on the other hand, become an important lesson increasing our curiosity and improving our intercultural awareness.

All people have the potential to develop their cultural intelligence if they want to. But people have different personalities, preferences, learning capacities, attitudes and ways of relating to other people, and it follows that they also have different ways of expressing their cultural intelligence and different potentials for developing it. People go into an intercultural meeting with different personal preferences, so they also respond differently to the same situation, and this results in different strengths and difficulties within the three dimensions of cultural intelligence.

Those who have experienced heterogeneous societies and environments in their lives will be used to people who think and act differently than they themselves do, and they may be expected to have a higher cultural intelligence than people who are used to homogeneous environments, and who have been able to run on autopilot, and therefore lack the same level of preparedness with respect to differences. But a life in a heterogeneous society can also have given them a feeling of the superiority of their own culture and stereotypic perceptions of people from other cultures.

Travelling to other countries can help to increase our own cultural intelligence, but this does not happen automatically. It depends on the extent to which, and on the ways in which, we come into contact with the people in the other country, and on what significance we attach to the differences which we observe. If we have only superficial contact with, for example, the service staff at meetings and in hotels, and no insight is gained into the lives and opinions of the country's inhabitants, it is quite possible to return home with a confirmation of the stereotypes which we held on departure. "They're really very friendly and hospitable", or "Yes, they have their systems which it's best to follow." The same applies in the workplace, for if we can't get below the surface of the stereotypes about other professions, there is a risk of reinforcing our preconceptions rather than developing our cultural intelligence.

What type of learning can develop cultural intelligence?

Cultural intelligence cannot be developed through what is called simple learning processes which concern acquiring new knowledge and new patterns of behaviour without changing one's understanding of the surroundings and of oneself. The development of cultural intelligence belongs to the complex learning processes where we learn how to learn, and where knowledge and understanding are transferred from one field to another. This is a type or learning where our 'map of the world' is rocked, and where it is necessary to revise our understanding of the surroundings and of ourselves. Complex learning requires learning situations where theory, observation, experimentation and experiences are combined and reflected upon.

When you plan activities for the development of cultural intelligence, it is necessary to ensure that a range of approaches is employed so that the brain, the body and the senses are all engaged. The design must allow rich opportunity for reflection during the process so it is possible to think about what has been experienced and learned, and how it should be used to learn more. The object of the activities must be clear, and it is necessary at intervals to go to meta-level and reflect upon what has been achieved, and what the next important step will be.

Cultural intelligence in summary form

The three dimensions of cultural intelligence were presented in Chapter 1 and the following résumé aims to give an overview.

Intercultural engagement

- The motivation to generate results together with people who are different from you. Interest in understanding the other party and making yourself understood.
- The ability to contain and handle your own and other people's

emotional reactions, knowing that the reactions can be culturally determined.

- The emotional maturity and mental flexibility to question your cultural self-knowledge and preconceptions about other people.
- A learning attitude, curiosity and the courage to allow yourself to be changed by the intercultural encounter.
- Being present, that is to say, creating rapport with the other person and being in contact with yourself and your reactions in the situation.

Cultural understanding

- Cultural self-awareness – that is, the ability to see yourself as a cultural being and knowing that your thoughts and actions can be culturally determined.
- An understanding of the other party – that is, general knowledge of cultural differences and specific knowledge of the other person's culture.
- Cultural understanding of the situation – that is, sensing and discovering that cultural differences are at play.
- The ability to extract experiences from one cultural encounter with, for example, focus on professional differences, and to transfer this learning to another type of cultural encounter where the focus might be on national or other differences.
- Flexibility in terms of understanding so that it is possible to see a situation from different cultural positions and in a broader perspective.

Intercultural communication

- The ability to turn off your cultural autopilot and revert to manual control – that is, to stop some of your own cultural routines and act to establish contact with the other party on common ground.

- The ability to move the conversation to meta-level – that is, to talk about how we talk so that the participants become attentive and can talk about the situation viewed a little from above, in a broader perspective.
- The ability to experiment in the situation and perhaps go beyond a threshold of embarrassment in order to move beyond habitual practices.
- The ability to be persistent, to focus on the possibilities in the situation and seek feedback.
- The ability to apply various communication tools for improving mutual contact and understanding in the cultural encounter.

Individual preparation for cultural encounters

Individuals can focus firmly on their cultural intelligence and create good conditions for their next cultural encounter, where they will be working together with people who think and act differently from themselves. Whether you are awaiting expatriation, joining an interdisciplinary project, participating in an international group, or doing better at a multicultural workplace or in a newly merged company, it is a good idea to prepare to contribute constructively. Preparation can be divided into the three CI dimensions, and the following can be used as a checklist. As the preparations must of course be tailored to the situation ahead, some of the questions below will be more relevant than others.

Checklist for the three dimensions of cultural intelligence
Intercultural engagement

- What is my motivation for going into this cultural encounter? How can I benefit from it? How can the company benefit from it?

- What experiences do I have from similar cultural encounters? How did I react? What emotions could conceivably underpin this situation? (Pride, taboos, power plays, previous experience of each other, what are the stakes in the situation). What could be my emotional pitfalls in this situation?
- Have I tried previously to explore my self-awareness in this field, and how did I find it? Do I have strong emotions about the other parties in the encounter?
- What can I learn in this encounter? What am I particularly curious about?
- How can I prepare myself for the situation and get all the professional details clear, so I can be as mentally present and flexible as possible in the situation, and not be distracted?

Cultural understanding

- Which of my cultural identities will come especially into play in the situation? I wonder how other parties perceive it when I express these identities.
- Are there cultural traits among the others to which I'll have to pay special attention? Things that are important for them?
- What cultural misunderstandings could we risk evoking if we're not careful? What will be the first signs that we understand or don't understand each other?
- Does this cultural encounter remind me of others I've experienced, and are there any experiences from them I can use in the present situation?
- What role can cultural differences possibly play in this situation? Are there differences of interest or power, or personal or other differences which should not be confused with cultural differences?

- Which of my cultural features and routine actions in particular should I try to stop using and instead switch to manual control in this situation?

- What are my options for introducing 'going to meta-level' in this encounter in relation to my role and task? How can I start it? Can I bring it up myself, or should I ally myself with others?

- What's the most awkward thing that could happen in this situation? What's the worst thing that could happen if an awkward situation develops?

- How important is it for me that this encounter is constructive? How much will I invest in the situation to make it succeed? Are there points I can concede to ease the situation?

- What processes, methods and questions could be useful to remember in this situation? Do any of them require that I have some specific information with me?

- What options do I have to turn the development of cultural intelligence into a joint project in this group so that it will become a part of the group's continuing activities?

These reflections increase our awareness of and readiness for the intercultural situation; they also take us through a number of considerations as a result of which we will be standing on firmer ground, and that in turn will enable us to be more flexible in the situation and more adventurous in exploring new routes for the creation of common ground in the encounter.

The optimal approach is to develop cultural intelligence through a joint effort with your partners so that your cultural differences and the way in which they are used are placed on the agenda for the cross-cultural situation you are in. Ideas for how cultural intelligence can be developed in groups and organisations are given later in this chapter.

Whether you develop cultural intelligence alone or as a member of a group, you can strengthen your learning experience from the situation by subsequently reflecting on what happened. What do I think after the meeting about the way things went? What are my thoughts when I compare my preparation with what actually happened? When was common ground created, and what made it happen? What did I contribute, and what was the result of trying new forms of communication? You can also go to meta-level and consider: How do I think about my thoughts after the situation?

The overview of the three CI dimensions can be used to assess what you yourself think you did best at the meeting, and which dimension you need to improve, in order to be able to make an even better contribution next time you go into the same or other intercultural situations. It's a question of using your experience in new situations and experimenting with ways of being culturally intelligent.

Why should organisations develop cultural intelligence?

There are many different situations where it can be useful for an organisation to develop cultural intelligence among its managers and employees. The purpose can be:

- To encourage more creative thinking and innovation among employees, either generally or as a lever in innovative processes.
- To promote cultural integration in a merger and initiate new and constructive cultural traits, both in national and in international mergers.
- To improve the quality of the collaboration in international,

interdisciplinary and inter-organisational project groups.

- To make international partnerships more effective and satisfactory for both old and new partners in different countries.
- To improve the working environment and revitalise partnerships across work areas, geographic location, ethnicity, education and other boundaries if they are marred by stereotypic perceptions of one another or if the first indications of conflict are emerging.
- To create a new orientation and work more effectively with its diversity management – whether the diversity is ethnic or broader.

The development of cultural intelligence can be directly targeted where professional contact between people with different cultural backgrounds either results in inappropriate friction or does not adequately produce the desired results.

Analysis of CI profile

A CI development process in a group will include assessment of where the group stands with respect to experiences of and attitudes to culture and cultural differences, and what their level and profile are in relation to the three dimensions of cultural intelligence. When culture is viewed as a process between people, and cultural intelligence as actual actions in a cultural encounter, the only sensible way to assess a person's or a group's cultural intelligence is via dialogue and interaction. A process must be designed for and aimed at analysing the level of the three CI dimensions. Games, case histories or other methods can be used to activate the participants and stimulate new kinds of conversations across cultural differences and within the groups. Managers and employees will thus analyse the same situation together, define the purpose of developing cultural intelligence, and decide what must be especially developed. How do the group members stand with regard to the different aspects of intercultural engagement? Where are the strengths and what needs to be especially developed? The same questions should be asked of the different aspects of cultural understanding and intercultural communication, and a profile of the group members' cultural intelligence will thus gradually be constructed.

Such a mutually engaging process of analysis will in itself contribute to the development of the group's cultural intelligence, for while the analysis is being made, a new awareness will emerge of the importance of culture for the partnership and its results, as well as a shared language which will make it easier to talk about it in the future. The interdependence of the three dimensions can be explored by sharing experiences from different cultural encounters and, through these reflections, new knowledge and ideas for learning activities will arise.

Principles for the development of cultural intelligence

Development of the organisation's cultural intelligence can proceed in big and small units, in short and long sequences and in very different contexts, but there are some general principles which always apply:

- Clear relevance for main task and performance. The development of cultural intelligence must be seen in relation to the organisation's vision and current strategy. What will cultural intelligence act as a lever for in relation to the main task, and what results are hoped for? This question gives direction and meaning to the process and it contributes to the building of common ground in the cultural encounter.
- Focus on the process – back to basics. To be able to access the

potential in intercultural groups, it is just as important to focus on the process as to focus on the content. Creating clear common ground and insight into the different cultural backgrounds requires management to switch off its autopilot and ensure that all participants are given an equal opportunity for contributing. When wanting to advance different experiences and points of view, nothing should be taken for granted beforehand, and this is a very good exercise in clear and targeted communication and plain management. It is important to explain the goals, balance the expectations against one another, clarify the ground rules for the partnership, check the understanding of expectations and goals, reflect upon the performance and the process, renegotiate methods, and gather new ideas.

- Avoid focusing on one single cultural difference. The way you frame and name issues will direct people's attention to certain aspects and therefore strongly influence the way people see things – it will create the reality in the situation. Whether the focus is on professional, national, organisational or other cultural differences in the development of cultural intelligence, it is very important to include other differences between those involved so that the significance of one category is not exaggerated, with the result of stereotyping and polarisation between groups. Look also at the differences between the people within the groups ('the cultures in cultures'), and create an awareness of other types of differences which may intersect the groupings in focus. In this way you help people to see the concrete cultural complexity and to see themselves and others as individuals with multiple cultural identities.

Using the models and tools

The concrete situation and the analysis of the group's CI profile will decide the location of the best starting point and the most suitable methods for development. The initiatives required will be different, according to whether intercultural engagement is high while intercultural communication is at beginners' level, or whether there is a high level of competence with respect to cultural understanding, but low intercultural engagement. There can also be big differences within an organisation's employees and job areas, and selected people should perhaps be key agents in the development of cultural intelligence. Development initiatives must have a clear purpose, but space must also be allowed in order to accommodate unforeseen learning situations.

Each of the three theme chapters presented models and tools for the development of cultural intelligence in groups and organisations, but these approaches can also be used in other cultural areas.

As was evident in the review of methods, all the approaches can have a positive effect on the development of more than one CI dimension. For example, an appreciative dialogue between two people will not merely lead to better contact and increased interest and curiosity in relation to the dialogue partner. It will also yield greater knowledge and understanding of each other's cultural background – and perhaps the two people will discover new ways of communicating across their mutual differences during the conversation. The design and the context of the dialogue determine which of the CI dimensions will be especially developed in the situation, and the same applies to the other tools. All approaches can therefore be used as the starting point for the development of any of the three CI dimensions, but for the sake of clarity we have listed the models and tools below according to the dimension to which each one is particularly suitable for opening the door.

If the starting point for the development of cultural intelligence is to be intercultural engagement, the following methods may, for example, be used:

- Opening the cultural field (Chapter 5)
- Appreciative dialogue (Chapter 4)
- Building relationships (Chapter 5).

If the starting point for development of the cultural intelligence is to be cultural understanding, the following methods and model may be used:

- Exploring important codes (Chapter 5)
- The cultural propeller (Chapter 3)
- Exploring culture (Chapter 4)
- A model for understanding – Culture Bridging Fundamentals© (Chapter 4).

If the starting point for development of cultural intelligence is to be intercultural communication, the following methods may, for example, be used:

- Ground rules (Chapters 4 and 5)
- Feedback (Chapter 5)
- Time for reflection and evaluation (Chapter 5).

Inspiration can be found in the following models and recommendations for general advice and the framework for development activities:

- Facilitation (Chapter 3)
- Support from a process consultant (Chapter 5)
- Model for groups' experience of similarities and differences (Chapter 3)
- Management's sponsorship (Chapter 3)
- Follow-up on and implementation of cultural traits (Chapter 4).

A development activity must always start by meeting the participants where they are, and it must be easy to see its relevance to the daily work, so use the possibilities available for development of cultural intelligence in daily life. For example, let it be a fixed part of the procedure for development projects that the group members investigate their differences and similarities in the starting phase and agree how they will use them throughout the project as well as what ground rules will help them forward towards a culturally intelligent partnership. Let the progress of cultural intelligence be a part of the fixed elements which are followed up in the various phases of the project. At the organisational level, this is only the first step. The next is to establish knowledge sharing for culturally intelligent project work. Let groups collect their experiences with the intercultural partnership so the next project group will not have to start from scratch to develop cultural intelligence. Good methods for developing cultural intelligence must be collected throughout the organisation in order to improve all types of cross-cultural work. For these are precious experiences, and they will be lost if the groups focus only on their work, and not on the processes and methods which produced the results.

References

Achen, Benedikte; Lande Andersen, Kristoffer; Donkin, Chris & Hinge, Marianne: *Tro, håb og tværfaglighed*. Thesis: Master of the Psychology of Organization, RUC 2003.

Adler, Nancy: *International Dimensions of Organizational Behaviors*. South-western College Publishing, 1997.

Amtoft, Mette & Vestergaard, Arne: "Ledelse i kompleksitet – 7 perspektiver på globale projektlederkompetencer". In *Erhvervspsykologi*, Vol. 1 No. 3, 2003.

Anneberg, Inger & Plum, Elisabeth: "Fusioner and opkøb: Virksomhedskulturen skal være en medspiller". *Ledelse i Dag*, No. 53, 2003.

Bourdieu, Pierre & Wacquant, Loïc: *An Invitation to Reflexive Sociology*. University of Chicago Press, 1992.

Dahl, Øyvind: *Møter mellom mennesker. Interkulturell kommunikasjon*. Gyldendal Akademisk, 2001.

Dale, Erling Lars: *Pædagogisk Filosofi*. Forlaget KLIM, 1999.

Darsø, Lotte: *Innovation in the Making*. Samfundslitteratur, 2001.

Darsø, Lotte: *Findes der en formel for innovation?* Børsens Håndbøger, 2003.

Davies, Bronwyn & Harré, Ron: "Positioning: The Discursive Production of Selves". In *Journal for the Theory of Social Behaviour*, Vol. 20, No. 1, 1990.

Dræby, Inger: *Breaking the Codes – Working with Cross-cultural Groups*. Lund, MIL-Concepts, 1999.

Earley, P.C.: "A theory of Cultural Intelligence in Organizations". In B.M. Staw & R.M. Kramer (Eds.) *Research in Organizational Behavior*, Vol. 24 pp. 271–99. Greenwich, CT: JAI Press, 2002.

Earley, P. Christopher & Ang, Soon: *Cultural Intelligence. Individual Interactions Across Cultures*. Stanford University Press, 2003.

Earley, P. Christopher; Ang, Soon & Tan, Joo-Seng: *CQ. Developing Cultural Intelligence at Work*. Stanford University Press, 2006.

Ely, Robin J.; Meyerson, Debra E. & Davidson, Martin N.: "Rethinking Political Correctness". *Harvard Business Review*, September 2006.

Erickson, Frederick: "Gatekeeping and the Melting Pot: Interaction in Counseling Encounters". In *Harvard Educational Review*, Vol. 45, No. 1, February 1995, Harvard University Press.

Erickson, Frederick & Schultz, Jeffrey: *The Counselor as Gatekeeper – Social Interaction in Interviews*. Academic Press, 1982.

Fiberline Composites: www.fiberline.dk.

Gancel, Charles et al.: *Successful Mergers, Acquisitions and Strategic Alliances*. McGraw-Hill, 2002.

Gardner, Howard: *Frames of Mind: The Theory of Multiple Intelligences*. Basic Books Inc., 1983.

Goleman, Daniel: *Emotional Intelligence: Why It Can Matter More Than IQ*. Bantam, 1995.

Goleman, Daniel: Working *with Emotional Intelligence*. Bantam, 1998.

Goleman, Daniel: *Social Intelligence. The new Science of Human Relations*. Random House, 2006.

Gumperz, John; Jupp, T.C. & Roberts, Celia: *Crosstalk – A study of Cross-Cultural Communication*, Background material and notes to accompany the B.B.C. film. The National Centre for Industrial Language Training, 1979.

Hall, Edward. *Beyond Culture*. Anchor Books, 1976/1989.

Hall, Edward T. & Hall, Mildred Reed: *Understanding Cultural Differences: Germans, French and Americans*. Intercultural Press, Inc., 1990.

Haslebo, Gitte: "Organisationskonsultation, når virksomheder fusioneres". In Haslebo, Gitte & Kit Sanne Nielsen: *Erhvervspsykologi In praksis*. Dansk Psykologisk Forlag, 1998.

Herlitz, Gillis: *Kultur Grammatik. Kunsten at møde andre kulturer*. Munksgaard, 1993.

Hofstede, Geert: *Cultures and Organizations – Intercultural Cooperation and Its Importance for Survival*. HarperCollinsBusiness, 1994.

Hofstede, Geert & Harris Bond, Michael: "The Confucius Connection: From Cultural Roots To Economic Growth". In *Organizational Dynamics* 16, 1988.

Hylland Eriksen, Thomas: *Etnicitet och nationalism*. Bokförlaget Nya Doxa, 2003.

Jacobs, Benedicte Lützen; Dorte Cohr & Plum, Elisabeth: *Mangfoldighed som virksomhedsstrategi – På vej mod den inkluderende organisation*. Gyldendal Uddannelse, 2001.

Jaffee, David: *Organizational theory – tension and change*. McGraw-Hill Publishing, 2001.

Jensen, Iben: *Grundbog i kulturforståelse*. Roskilde Universitetsforlag, 2005.

Jensen, Iben: *Hvornår er man lige kvalificeret? Etniske minoriteters professionelle adgang til etablerede danske medier*. Nævnet for Etnisk Ligestilling, 2000.

Jensen, Iben: *Interkulturel kommunikation i komplekse samfund*. Roskilde Universitetsforlag, 1998.

Jensen, Iben (2002): "Kulturel kompetence". Bidrag til Det Nationale

Kompetenceregnskab, see www.nkr.dk.

Justesen, Susanne: *Innoversity – The dynamic Relationship between Innovation and Diversity*. København Business School, Working paper, 2000.

Kleppestø, Stein: *Kultur och identitet vid företagsuppköp och fusioner*. Nerenius & Santèrus Förlag, 1993.

Klinker, Sabine & Hvorslef Rasmussen, Marie: "Forestillede forskelle". In *Dansk Sociologi* Vol. 17, No. 2, September 2006.

Lauvås, Kirsti & Per: *Tværfagligt samarbejde – perspektiv and strategi*. Forlaget KLIM, 1998.

Lewin, Kurt: "Some Social-Psychological Differences between the United States and Germany". In *Journal of Personality* 4 (4), 265–93, 1936.

Lindholm, Mikael R. & Møller, Kim: *Slip innovationen løs*. Børsens Forlag, 2004.

Liversage, Annika: *Finding a path – Labour market life stories of professional immigrants*. Doctoral thesis, Copenhagen Business School, 2006.

Martin, Joanne: *Organizational Culture. Mapping the Terrain*. Sage Publications, 2002.

Maturana, H. & Varela, F.: *The Tree of Knowledge*. Revised Edition, Shambhala, 1987/1992.

Molin, Jan & Strandgaard Pedersen, Jesper: *Fusioner i Danmark*. Handelshøjskolens Forlag, 1996.

Norlyk, Birgitte: "Fagkultur and organisation som jokere – efteruddannelse af blandede målgrupper". *Tidsskrift for universiteternes efter- and videreuddannelse*, No. 8, 2006.

Ofman, Daniel: *Kernekvaliteter – organisationens skjulte værdier*. Jyllands-Postens Forlag, 2002.

Olson, Gary M. & Olson, Judith S.: "Distance Matters". In *Human-Computer Interaction*, 2000, Vol. 15. Lawrence Erlbaum Associates, 2006.

Peterson, Brooks: *Cultural Intelligence: A Guide to Working with People from Other Cultures*. Intercultural Press, 2004.

Plum, Elisabeth: "Evaluering af projekt etnisk rekruttering". EU, *The Information, The Politiken, The JydskeVestkysten*, Sjællandske Medier and the Danish Broadcasting Corporation, channel DR, 2003. (Can be downloaded from www.plum.co.dk.)

Plum, Elisabeth: "Mangfoldighedsledelse – dynamikken mellem ligestilling and ressourcer". In *Med kurs mod mangfoldighed. Begreber og praksis i integrationsindsatsen*. Hans Reitzels Forlag, 2004. Also published in *Erhvervspsykologi*, Vol. 4, No. 1, March 2006.

Poulsen, Per Thygesen: "M & A: fra eufori til skepsis and eftertanke". *Ledelse i Dag*, No. 53, 2003

Qvortrup, Lars: *Det vidende samfund*. Forlaget Unge Pædagoger, 2004.

Rasmussen, Palle: Kreativ og innovativ kompetence 1. In *Nøglekompetencer – forskerbidrag til det nationale kompetenceregnskab*, 2002. Can be downloaded from the website of the Danish Ministry of Education (Undervisningsministeriet).

Rohlin, Lennart et al. (Eds.): *Earning while Learning in Global Leadership*. Lund, MiL Publishers, 2002.

Schein, Edgar: *Organizational culture and leadership: A dynamic view*. Jossey-Bass, 1985. In Danish: *Organisationskultur and ledelse*. Forlaget Valmuen, 1994.

Scheuer, Jann: *Den umulige samtale – sprog, køn and magt i jobsamtaler*. Akademisk forlag, 1998.

Shaw, Patricia: *Intervening in the shadow systems of organizations*. CMC paper. University of Hertfordshire, 2002.

Skovholm, Jens: *Et spørgsmål om kultur*. Dansk Flygtningehjælp, 2005.

Stacey, Ralph: *Complexity and Creativity in Organizations*. Berrett-Koehler, 1996.

Staunæs, Dorthe: Køn, etnicitet and skoleliv. Samfundslitteratur, 2004.

Strøier, Vibe: "Fusionernes Oxymoroner – Håb og Vemod i Mellemtiden". In *Erhvervspsykologi*, Vol. 4, No. 2, June 2006.

Søderberg, Anne-Marie & Vaara, Eero (Ed.): *Merging Across Borders. People, Cultures and Politics*. Copenhagen Business School Press, 2003.

Søndergaard, Dorte Marie: *Tegnet på kroppen – køn, koder and konstruktioner blandt unge voksne In Akademia*. Museum Tusculanum, 1996.

Thomas, David C. & Inkson, Kerr: *Cultural Intelligence. People Skills for Global Business*. Berrett-Koehler Publishers, 2004.

Trompenaars, Fons & Hampden-Turner, Charles: *Riding the Waves of Culture*. Nicholas Brealey Publishing, 1997.

Vestergaard, Arne: *Non-determinist vocabularies of coping with complex conditions for managers of projects, development and change in organizations*. www.under skoven.dk, 2005.

Weber, Max: *Die protestantische Ethik und der "Geist" der Kapitalismus*. 1905. Beltz Athenäum, 2000.

Weiss, Kirsten: *Når vikinger slås*. Jyllands-Postens Forlag, 2006.

Zimmerman, Brenda (2001): *Ralph Stacey's Agreement & Certainty Matrix*. York University, Toronto, 2001. www.plexusinstitute.org/edgeware/archive/think/main_aides3.html.

Authors

Elisabeth Plum has spent all her working life on the question of how the differences between people can be bridged, and how these differences can be turned to an advantage. She has worked with company mergers, international groups, diversity management, and cross-disciplinary project groups. She also works as an independent consultant in the field of management development and change management in the private and public sectors. She holds a PhD in cultural sociology, and before starting her own consultancy in 1995, she worked as a research fellow at Roskilde University and as an internal organisational consultant in Danish companies. Elisabeth Plum is a visiting professor at Middlesex University Business School (London) and an associate partner of the international consultancy Inter Cultural Management Associates in France. She has published several articles and books on cultures and merger management and other topics.
Website: **www.culturalintelligence.org**

Benedikte Achen is a management consultant. Since 1995, she has had her own consultancy, where she works with management development and processes of change. She is particularly interested in how knowledge workers are successfully managed, and how innovative processes are created in projects. The relationship between personal leadership and establishment of sustainable roles and relations in the organisation is another area of focus. Benedikte Achen is affiliated with the Danish Centre for Public Competence Development, where she works with the in-service training of managers. She has a background in ethnology and holds an MA in organisational psychology, and she is co-author of a number of articles and books on management and professional dialogues in the workplace. Website: **www.benedikteachen.dk**

Inger Dræby holds a PhD in comparative literature and is an independent consultant. She has been working for over 20 years as a process consultant for a number of Nordic and international companies including 3M, Volvo, IKEA, GKN and Coop Norden. She is affiliated with the MiL Institute in Sweden, ICM Associates in France, and the consultancy network conSense in Denmark. Inger Dræby suffered her first culture shock when she moved from provincial Denmark to Copenhagen, and another when she moved from public service to private business. Her interest in organisational culture has since become a guide wire in her professional work, supplemented by studies of national differences and conflict handling. Website: **www.draeby.dk**

Iben Jensen is associate professor at Roskilde University. She holds a PhD in cultural sociology and a PhD in communication. She has been carrying out research and teaching in intercultural communication at Roskilde University Centre for 15 years and she has been an active speaker outside the University throughout this period. She has held courses and given lectures on intercultural competence, cultural understanding and the professional cultural encounter as it develops in such diverse professional groups as dentists, the clergy and human resources employees. Iben Jensen has published numerous articles and books on her subject, most importantly *Introduction to Cultural Understanding* (2007). She has edited *Bridges of Understanding – Perspectives on Intercultural Communication* (2006), a reader, with Professor Øyvind Dahl and Peter Nynäs.

Index

Middlesex University

VITAL DIFFERENCES

A GLOBAL PROGRAMME DESIGNED FOR BUSINESS LEADERS TO ENHANCE THEIR ABILITY TO WORK IN CULTURALLY COMPLEX ENVIRONMENTS

This programme is aimed at thought leaders and senior executives in private, public and international organisations whose role demands skill in bridging and benefiting from cultural diversity across nationality, organisational culture and work discipline.

A NEW WAY OF THINKING AND WORKING

The challenges and problems of culturally complex organisations cannot be solved using the models of the 20th century. It is necessary to develop a new mindset and way of working that assumes difference so that we can use differences to develop new ideas, solve complex problems and benefit from diversity.

Vital Differences is based on the concept of Cultural Intelligence which we believe is one of the key competencies for future leaders. This programme is designed as a unique learning opportunity and delivers a challenging and enjoyable development experience.

The facilitation, teaching and administration are provided by Middlesex University Business School and supported by guest speakers and companies based in the particular region for each workshop location. To find out more please visit: **www.mdx.ac.uk/vitaldifferences**

MIDDLESEX UNIVERSITY
BUSINESS SCHOOL

Middlesex University Business School is one of four schools which make up Middlesex University. The Business School has been offering high-quality business education for over fifty years and has an international portfolio of programmes, taught in different locations around the world. Our students and faculty come from 160 different countries. We offer MBA programmes, customised executive education and continuing professional development to our clients around the world.

THE LEARNING EXPERIENCE

Middlesex University Business School prides itself on its practical, innovative and flexible approach to executive development on the needs of the business. We use different methods to meet different needs including:

Case Studies: using practical, real life examples bringing theory to life and encouraging active participation and collective engagement with business problems.

Action Learning: a process whereby the participants study their own actions and experiences in order to improve performance. It enables each person to reflect and review the action they have taken and the learning points which have arisen.

Work Based Learning and Accreditation of Learning: Middlesex University has pioneered this method of learning whereby we collect and recognise the learning which takes place in the work environment. We believe that the most valuable learning takes place outside the classroom, in the workplace, through life experiences and we have developed a learning framework based on this principle.

Middlesex University Business School works with a wide range of companies and businesses in the private and public sectors to develop and deliver tailor-made accredited programmes for all levels of staff. Please visit **www.mdx.ac.uk/bs**